SUPERVISORY MANAGEMENT

For a complete list of Management Books 2000 titles,
visit our web-site on http://www.mb2000.com

SUPERVISORY MANAGEMENT

Sidney Callis

For Bim ... for everything.

Copyright © Sidney Callis 2003

All rights reserved. No part of this publication may be reproduced, stored in a retrieval system, or transmitted in any form or by any means, electronic, mechanical, photocopying, recording, or otherwise without the prior permission of the publishers.

First published in 2003 by Management Books 2000 Ltd
Forge House, Limes Road
Kemble, Cirencester
Gloucestershire, GL7 6AD, UK
Tel: 0044 (0) 1285 771441/2
Fax: 0044 (0) 1285 771055
E-mail: m.b.2000@virgin.net
Web: mb2000.com

Printed and bound in Great Britain by Biddles, Guildford

This book is sold subject to the condition that it shall not, by way of trade or otherwise, be lent, resold, hired out, or otherwise circulated without the publisher's prior consent in any form of binding or cover other than that in which it is published and without a similar condition including this condition being imposed upon the subsequent purchaser.

British Library Cataloguing in Publication Data is available
ISBN 1-85252-420-0

Contents

PREFACE   9

CHAPTER 1   11
A philosophical introduction
To get you thinking: Company and job knowledge – what do you know?   17

CHAPTER 2 – ABOUT SUPERVISION   21
What is a Supervisor?; Discipline; What the Supervisor needs to know; The purpose of a Supervisor; A profile of the ideal Supervisor; The Supervisor as leader
To get you thinking: Frustration factors; Frustration factors – commentary   30

CHAPTER 3 – LEADERSHIP   32
Need for leadership; Characteristics of a good leader; Types of authority; Leader versus Driver; Leadership and group management
To get you thinking: Thinking about leadership; Leadership Quiz – Commentary   40

CHAPTER 4 – ORGANISATION AND PLANNING   42
Organising your team; Planning
To get you thinking: Thinking about planning   48

CHAPTER 5 – CONTROLLING   50
What is control?; Supervisory control; Accountability; Management by objectives; Control systems
To get you thinking: Control checklist; Control checklist – commentary   57

CHAPTER 6 – PROBLEM SOLVING   59
Introduction; How to define and handle problems – a six-step process; An important tool to assist problem solving; Problem solving ideas
To get you thinking: To help you think about problem solving   68

CHAPTER 7 – TIME MANAGEMENT   69
Managing your time; Some Time Management principles; The Pareto principle; Time wasters
To get you thinking: Do you have time management problems?   78

CHAPTER 8 – TIME BUDGETING   80
The time budget – an important time management technique; Projects and time management; Hints on self organisation; Action meetings
To get you thinking: What makes a good time manager?; What makes a good time manager – commentary   89

CHAPTER 9 – MANAGING CHANGE   92
Managing change; Essential considerations in managing change; Management style and change; Authoritative and Participative management styles – advantages and disadvantages
To get you thinking: Checklist for the management of change   97

CHAPTER 10 – DELEGATION   98
Introduction; The Story of Moses; Reasons why supervisors do not delegate; The delegation process; Effective delegation; Delegation advantages; What/what not to delegate
To get you thinking: Checklist for delegation   106

CHAPTER 11 – COMMUNICATION SKILLS   107
The communication process; Communication barriers; Types of barrier; Overcoming communication barriers; Written or spoken communication? Using questions creatively; Listening skills
To get you thinking: Keys to effective listening   118

CHAPTER 12 – NON-VERBAL COMMUNICATION   119
Body Language
To get you thinking: Try this to get a grip on body language   122

Contents

CHAPTER 13 – EFFECTIVE MEETINGS 123
Meetings, bloody meetings!; before the meeting; During the Meeting; After the meeting
To get you thinking: Checklist for successful meetings; Checklist for running the meeting 128

CHAPTER 14 – PRESENTATION SKILLS 130
Introduction; What the listener sees and hears; Good delivery; Presentation planning; The 'Basic Relevance' Test; Notes
To get you thinking: How to sharpen your presentation skills 137

CHAPTER 15 – MOTIVATION AND EXPECTATIONS 138
Motivation in the work situation; Practical steps in motivation; Motivation theories; Ways to effectively demotivate; Create the right climate; Expectations
To get you thinking: Motivation – subordinates; Motivation – subordinates: commentary 151

CHAPTER 16 – HUMAN RELATIONS 154
Human relationships
To get you thinking: Human relations – How I rate myself; Human relations: commentary 158

CHAPTER 17 – COACHING 161
Coaching defined; The coaching process; Coaching skills
To get you thinking: Your coaching style 171

CHAPTER 18 – CONCLUSION 174

FURTHER READING 177

Figures in the text:

1.	Task Group & Individual Needs	38
2.	The Planning Triangle	45
3.	The Control Cycle	52
4.	Cause & Effect	63
5.	Pareto Principle	73
6.	The Time-waster Puzzle	74
7.	A Var Chart	84
8.	Action Statement	87
9.	Management Styles & Change	94
10.	Moses: Organisation Chart	99
11.	The Delegation Process	101
12.	Communication Barriers	108
13.	Maslow – Hierarchy of Needs	142
14	Theory X and theory Y	144
15.	Herzberg – Motivation & Hygiene Factors	145
16.	The Coaching Process	163

Preface

Many people have helped me write this book; dozens of authors, whose wisdom I have absorbed; scores of managers, supervisors, directors and business leaders, whose experience I have profited from; and many hundreds of students to whom I have tried to pass on my perceptions of how to manage. I must also admit to my own debt to myself in recycling some of my own previous writings, especially in time management, communication, meetings, delegation and more.

Some of my inspirers are mentioned in the text; others will be found in the suggested further reading. But the book is more than my interpretations of other people's thoughts; I have also done a lot of lengthy thinking myself, some of which is contained in the first chapter.

Management at supervisory level is a difficult balancing act. On the one hand there is the duty to carry out orders and ensure that the job is done. On the other, is the obligation to be creative in getting the job done with maximum effectiveness, but often without the authority to implement the innovations which would bring improved performance.

This book looks at what the supervisor does; what they could do if only ... and also helps to move the aspirations a little forward with helpful exercises, checklists, self evaluations and reminders. These will be found following each chapter. Use them to fix the ideas of the chapter in your mind.

Also you may be able to use these exercises as training tools for developing your subordinates. Remember, a major (and generally unwritten) part of the supervisor's job is to develop staff. Hopefully, this book will assist in this task and of course your own development too.

I feel sure that you will enjoy reading this book and that there will be at least a few 'ah-ha's' when you come across some idea or practical point that you had not known about before. So welcome to 'Supervisory Management'; you are starting on an interesting trip. By the time you get to the other end, you will surely know a lot more about supervision and management.

Sidney Callis
Buckingham
February 2003

On a matter of style – it is obviously clear that supervisors can equally be male or female. Generally we have tried to avoid excessive use of 'he or she', although occasionally it is inevitable. If you see a 'he' or a 'she' on its own, then please imagine the opposite gender also.

1
A Philosophical Introduction

Management is a relatively recent phenomenon. Of course, there have always been bosses – from Moses, through Attila the Hun and Ghengis Khan, right down to the heroes (or villains) of our present time. Managing is getting things done through people; bosses get things done, often without consulting people at all. A mixture of intimidation, coercion and downright violence may be used; people were once treated as chattels, even slaves. One still sees remnants of these attitudes in the behaviour of some present-day managers.

Management implies that people matter. It has been dawning on enlightened bosses and thinkers that people work better, produce more and riot less, if they are treated with consideration of their humanity. The ideas of management have been accumulating steadily from the early 19th Century. Today, what we are involved in is a highly organised and sophisticated system that expends a vast amount of time, energy and other resources in 'getting things done through people'. Nowadays people count; they are the most important resource in any enterprise, whether commercial or not for profit, whether industrial or agricultural, whether big or small – people matter. Which is what this book is about – management and people.

The process of getting things done is arranged by people who work in a fairly general hierarchical pattern. The organisation of management is similar, whatever field of endeavour it is engaged in, from the armed forces to scientific research. Someone is chief; someone reports (i.e. is commanded by) to them; a further someone reports to the second in command and so on, right down to the lowliest office junior. Somewhere in this organisation comes the supervisor – for the supervisor is a manager, albeit with less responsibility or authority than the boss, but nonetheless charged with getting things done. These 'things' may be defined, closely or loosely or maybe not at all. But whereas the big boss has ultimate responsibility for everything in the organisation, the supervisor's is for a specified small area. This is why it is so important to have a clear statement of responsibilities and authority; without this, the supervisor may not be able to perform effectively. Sadly this clear statement is often missing.

So the supervisor is part of the chain of management, and it is a difficult part. Above is the boss, who may not have exactly specified the job (or may not be able to). Below are the workers, the subordinates who expect guidance and direction. Here is another difficulty: the supervisor may, indeed generally has, come from the ranks of the workers, having done the job well – thus the boss has promoted him or her. Very motivational – but it could be a disaster for the individual. Being a supervisor is a lonely job; your mates may envy you, or ridicule you, or subtly undermine you; your boss expects you to get the job done, without much help. Did you know what you were letting yourself in for; or have you had any training for this? Most unlikely on both counts.

Managing other people is a technique (art? science?) that can be taught and learned. Surprisingly, although there are innumerable management schools, they don't really teach the things that we deal with in this book. The theory of management is expounded in a remote 'hands off' way. In this book, we deal with the essential things of every day working life at the sharp end.

The things the supervisor needs to know concern the technical aspects of getting the job done and how best to get people to do it. The first things to understand are **where the supervisor fits, what is the role, and how personal leadership can be developed**. Without an understanding of these elements, any supervisor will be on shaky ground. Knowing what one's responsibilities are, within the context of the organisation, helps the individual to deal with the job effectively. Having a good idea of what leadership is about enables the supervisor to put some of the principles into practice and self develop

A Philosophical Introduction

– and also develop the staff.

Then there are the nuts and bolts of management – planning, controlling and problem solving. These things are a structural part of the supervisor's daily work. Everybody plans to some extent, but the supervisor has to plan, not just for his or her own activity, but for the team as well and also to meet the objectives of the organisation. This can be complex; integrating all the interests that are involved needs skill and determination. Then, it is essential to ensure that the plans are carried out; that the results planned for have actually happened. This again requires skill, because the idea of control can often be distasteful to some people.

Solving problems is often what the supervisor is most concerned with. It takes time which mostly is not a necessary expenditure of this valuable resource. The supervisor needs to be available to help with problem solving, whether it be a technical problem or a personal one. But the supervisor's attitude should be 'don't bring me problems, bring me answers'. In other words, don't ask me to solve problems which you can really solve yourself; and think about it a bit before yelling for me.

These aspects of the job are all time-consuming and therefore the effective supervisor will learn how to ration time and use it productively. We all of us 'waste' so much of our time, so that we get to the end of a day not having done half of what we intended to do! We outline some of the reasons for this and offer some ideas to help cope with 'lack of time'. We all have the same amount of time; some of us use what we have rather better (or worse) than others. If we have a job to do, in a specific amount of time, then we need to plan and control what we are doing, so that excessive problem solving does not hold us up.

Change happens all the time and the supervisor is called upon to manage it. Change of any sort can be upsetting, not just to the supervisor but to the staff also. How change is handled is a matter of management style. If people are considered when change is proposed or in progress, then the change is more likely to happen smoothly. If, on the other hand, change is imposed and people are not considered, then anxiety is evident, obstruction occurs, the 'we don't want/don't like this' syndrome shows strongly. The thinking supervisor will adapt his or her management style to the circumstances and call up leadership, planning and control skills. Also, good communication is vital in change situations; we look at this skill in detail later on. One important aspect of management style is the extent to which the supervisor is able/willing to delegate. Effective delegation extends the supervisor's capabilities as well as developing subordinate staff. Staff who are accustomed to extended delegation will be much more attuned to the difficulties of making changes, than those who simply accept orders.

We are beginning to see that the art of management is intricately tied up with the techniques of getting things done and using people to do things. Management is a structure of many parts; leave out one, or ignore, or miss, a piece and the thing goes lopsided. It may work, but not efficiently. Instead of a well-oiled machine which performs to specification, one may have a creaky ill-tempered beast which needs constant attention and adjustment to make it go at all. So many businesses are like the latter image and, if the supervisor's job is in amongst these creaks and groans, it is a difficult one. Thus, the thinking supervisor will do well to acquire and practice good management skills.

The ability to communicate effectively is one of the most potent skills that any individual can have in life. For the supervisor who must communicate both up to senior management and down to subordinates, having such a skill is a great asset. And communication skills can be learned, but they need a lot of determination and persistent practice. We talk mostly about spoken communicating because this is most of the supervisor's work: giving instructions; discussing plans or activity; making a presentation to explain, or to convince people about change. Most of this is the spoken word. The supervisor must also be skilled in the written word: for reports to be made, or plans to be drawn up and so on. This needs clarity of expression on paper. And there are other skills that the supervisor would do well to acquire: how to read body language; how to conduct a meeting effectively; questioning techniques to get the information that one needs; and learning to listen. This last skill is almost more

A Philosophical Introduction

important that speaking, or writing in a management context (or in life – apparently it is difficult for men to listen, less so for women!).

Without good communication skills, the quality of the supervisor's job will inevitably be less than optimum. Effectiveness will be measurably enhanced with improvement in communication skill. The supervisor has to deal with other people; it is thus important to understand what motivates people and how and why they form relationships. It is also helpful in the work situation to be able to perceive what people expect of us, and even more, what we expect of them – and how we show or express this. A level of sensitivity is called for to appreciate what motivates ourselves and those with whom we have to work. Well-motivated staff perform well; it is our job as supervisor to ensure that the level of motivation is high and that relationships within the work environment are smooth. Ruffled feathers spell trouble; low morale and poor motivation means poor results in the supervisor's work area. The figures do not lie: if there is a downturn in productivity, look for the causes, not in machine or materials failure, but in people failures.

This is where the supervisor's role as coach can have such a significant impact. Any supervisor accumulates a store of knowledge, wisdom and people skills. To make a difference, all these can be brought to bear in the process of coaching and helping: 'Let me help you do it' but not 'Let me do it for you'. The coach combines the functions of demonstrator, observer, commentator, evaluator and praiser. In all these areas, the supervisor as coach has the experience to guide individuals to satisfactory performance.

Each of the chapters of this book deals with the aspects of management that we have outlined. But important though these subjects are, there are many more areas of management about which the supervisor should know, but which will have little impact on the work, and which the supervisor will not be able to influence directly.

The supervisor will need to have some understanding of: finance, a vast and terrifying area for some; marketing, an arcane jungle; production; procurement; industrial relations and law, and much more. All this buzzes around the concept of 'management". And to supplement this are the latest fads, gimmicks and techniques dreamed up by consultants and academics in business schools, which often have no relevance or reality: 'Total Quality Management', 'Corporate Reengineering', to name but a couple of the most recent. The fads come and go; they flourish, then wither, then the next one arrives. The supervisor may be involved in the upheavals (change or chaos?) and that is part of the job. But the fundamentals that we outline in this book remain; they may get called by fancy names for some time but nevertheless they remain the basics of the supervisor's job.

Before you read any further it might be a good idea to take stock of what you know about your employer, how you fit in, and your job. Obviously, whatever you put into the questionnaire remains private to you. However, the most interesting thing is what you don't put in, i.e. what you don't know. It could really be worthwhile to fill in those gaps.

There are 40 questions but it is NOT an exam! There are no right or wrong answers – only what you know. Some points can be answered with a tick in the appropriate box, some require a few words in writing. We have left the appropriate spaces. If you don't know anything about a particular point, just leave it blank. But this could be an incentive for you to find out. Be assured, the questionnaire is simply for you to use if you wish to find out what you know and understand about your employers and your own job.

A Philosophical Introduction

To get you thinking:

Company and job knowledge – what do you know?

1) Company knowledge

1. What is the main purpose of your company?
   _____
   _____

2. What service does it provide, and to whom?
   _____
   _____

3. What does your section contribute to this?
   _____
   _____

4. What type of company is it?
   Public ☐   Private ☐   Partnership ☐   Sole Trader ☐

5. What did your company's last accounts show?
   Profit ☐   Loss ☐   Don't know how to read accounts ☐

6. What are your conditions of employment (holidays, overtime, etc.)?
   _____
   _____

7. What is the company's policy on staff committees, joint consultation, etc.?
   _____
   _____

8. Do trade unions or staff associations have any role in the company?
   _____

2) Where do you fit in?

1. To whom are you immediately responsible?

   Title: _____

2. To whom do you report in their absence?

   Title: _____

3. Can you trace the line of authority from yourself to the top and bottom of the company? Yes ☐ No ☐
4. Is the line clear? Yes ☐ No ☐
5. How many employees are responsible to you? Number: _____
6. Is this a manageable number? Yes ☐ No ☐
7. If not, what do you do about it?

   _____

   _____

8. Do you have regular contact with your manager?

   Yes ☐ No ☐

9. Who is your deputy who acts in your absence?

   Title: _____

10. What do your fellow supervisors do?

    _____

    _____

11. Do you meet with them regularly? Yes ☐ No ☐
12. Do you know the specialists in your company?

    Personnel Yes ☐ No ☐   Training Yes ☐ No ☐
    Accounts Yes ☐ No ☐   (tick those known, add others.)

    _____

    _____

3) Is this your job?

		Yes	No
1.	Determining the number of staff required in your section	☐	☐
2.	Selecting new staff	☐	☐
3.	Induction of new staff	☐	☐
4.	Training staff on the job	☐	☐
5.	Authorising leave of absence	☐	☐
6.	Arranging overtime	☐	☐
7.	Recommending merit awards	☐	☐
8.	Ensuring compliance with relevant statutory regulations	☐	☐
9.	Keeping various records	☐	☐
10.	Making staff reports	☐	☐
11.	Suggesting improved methods of working	☐	☐
12.	Keeping a check on costs and wastage	☐	☐
13.	Checking work	☐	☐
14.	Upgrading performance	☐	☐
15.	Keeping an eye on adequacy and effectiveness of furniture and equipment	☐	☐
16.	Supervising maintenance, cleaning and storage of items	☐	☐
17.	Keeping up to date with new ideas and new equipment and recommending their use where advisable	☐	☐
18.	Controlling flow of work through section	☐	☐
19.	Maintaining working team	☐	☐
20.	Planning for the future	☐	☐
21.	Making decisions about technical, organisational and human problems	☐	☐

Looking at this list, is your workload:

    too much? ☐   too little? ☐

    enough to keep you busy without stress? ☐

Do you feel you have:

    adequate knowledge   Yes ☐ No ☐

    sufficient training   Yes ☐ No ☐

    to do the job?

**Think about what you have put in the questionnaire.
Do you feel you know enough about your job and who you work for?**

If you have left spaces unanswered, then, as you read through this book, maybe they will be filled in. Or maybe you will feel the need to go and find some answers.

Good hunting!

2

About Supervision

'I like work; it fascinates me. I can sit and look at it for hours.'
Jerome K Jerome

What is a Supervisor?

An overall definition of a supervisor is:

A member of the second line of management, responsible for a work group to a higher level of management.

They are therefore sometimes labelled 'second echelon management'. The supervisor's job has a technical element (knowledge of the product or service); and a managerial element. So supervisors have also been described as:

People who control the activities of others and are responsible for carrying out the intentions of management.

In order that this can occur effectively, supervisors must be:

- properly selected and trained

- have charge of a work group of a suitable size

- be fully briefed in advance about management's policies as they affect the work group

- be a close link in the exchange of information between management and the work group.

The job is to achieve objectives through the people for whom they are responsible. If a supervisor gets things done through people, success can be measured by the ability to get others to work effectively. What is required to do this? What abilities are needed?

The supervisor must:

- be in charge of a work group of 15 people or less, so that they can be treated as individuals and accept delegation effectively

- enjoy the trust and confidence of the group

- be able to tell them in advance about policies or changes that will affect them

- have good working relations

- take risks where necessary, yet be patient

- ensure that the group is well organised and trained to do the job

- set up excellent communications with their staff, their colleagues and their boss

- accept the responsibilities of leadership.

Discipline

One of a supervisor's chief responsibilities is for discipline. But what is discipline?

Whenever people work together, there must be certain rules; some personal freedom may need to be sacrificed in order to get the job

About Supervision

done. Without order there would not be efficiency.

Discipline is often expressed in terms of **reward and punishment**. The assumption is that only carrot and stick will persuade people to keep to the rules. This is really the failure of discipline; if we expect the worst from our staff, we are likely to get it. Conversely, if we treat staff fairly and with understanding, we will get a fair measure of loyalty and obedience in return.

Discipline is not domination. People will accept rules and conditions if they can see the reasons for them, and if they are just. Positive control is a system of accepted behaviour, not an imposed behaviour and needs to be worked at by the supervisor.

What the Supervisor needs to know

☑ Job knowledge

A thorough knowledge of the work which is being done by the team is essential. Also, the supervisor must have a clear understanding of his or her responsibilities. The section and the people who work in it are not an isolated unit; they form part of a larger team – the organisation as a whole. The supervisor needs to have a good knowledge of the company, its aims and its standards. The supervisor has to work within the policies of the company; to be effective he or she needs to be familiar with them.

☑ Accountability

Any company's organisation chart tends to oversimplify. Things are never quite so straightforward as they seem. It is important for the supervisor, and the staff, that they have a clear idea of where they belong in the organisation. Supervisors often have little idea precisely what their job entails.

☑ Job description

No one can work effectively unless they know what the job is. In some organisations, there may be a written detailed job description, in others only a general directive. The important thing is that supervisors need to be clear in their own minds about the responsibilities and the extent of their authority. Also effectiveness is increased if the boss is clear about the responsibilities and authority of the supervisor.

It is often difficult to get a comprehensive list of the responsibilities of the supervisor. If a written job description does not exist, the supervisor should write down their perception of what the responsibilities are. Then ask the boss to set down what they think the job is. The results will be rewarding and enlightening.

☑ Job responsibilities

The effectiveness of a supervisor is directly related to his or her use of time. Here are some pointers about the supervisor's job itself.

❖ **Accept objectives and policies**

Once these have been agreed, they should be accepted and not argued about every time they need to be considered. Policies should be challenged, but at the right time and in a proper manner.

❖ **Subdivide objectives**

Break down the overall objective into sub-objectives or short-term objectives for yourself and each subordinate.

❖ **Plan and programme**

Plan ahead on how the objectives are to be met. Agree on programmes with subordinates (what?/who?/by when?).

❖ **Implement**

Implementation includes organising and directing people, co-ordinating and communicating with other departments, modifying plans where required.

❖ **Control**

Control implementation by comparing actual achievement with plans and taking appropriate action.

About Supervision

❖ **Develop and train**
As a part of the day-to-day work, develop and train subordinates so that they become better able to accept more delegated responsibility and are ready for promotion sooner.

These points will be dealt with as we go on. They are briefly mentioned here so as to understand the broad responsibilities of the supervisor's job.

The purpose of a Supervisor

The purpose of a supervisor can be defined as:

To be responsible for the smooth running and production of the goods or services under their control through the resources available to them.

People involved in any activity require a *common point of reference* so that they do not lose direction in trying to achieve their objectives. This common point is the work group leader – the supervisor/manager/leader who guides people towards the aims and objectives of the organisation.

People are the most crucial of all the resources of an organisation. To many people their supervisor is the company. Supervisors are involved at some level in all the following functions:

- ✓ planning
- ✓ problem solving
- ✓ costing
- ✓ delegation
- ✓ evaluation
- ✓ organising
- ✓ cost control
- ✓ interviewing
- ✓ selection
- ✓ industrial relations

- ✓ discipline
- ✓ setting targets
- ✓ counselling
- ✓ standards
- ✓ appraisal
- ✓ training
- ✓ human relations
- ✓ communication
- ✓ co-ordination
  ... ... the list goes on.

These are of course the areas in which managers operate. The implication is that supervisors are managers. **This is often not recognised by their own managers, colleagues, subordinates and, most significantly, by the supervisors themselves!** This is one result of the enormous changes that have taken place in management in the last half of the twentieth century

Supervisors are the focal point of pressures resulting from changes of company policy and market needs. Reorganisation of management and trade unions has improved working conditions and wages. But this has also increased external influence in areas previously traditionally handled by the supervisors. People below, above and at the same level often fail to recognise the supervisor or show any respect. So supervisors are often the lost 'people in the middle", The role and purpose of supervisors has become blurred.

But the importance of the supervisor cannot be emphasised too strongly. This is particularly true when we take into account the need for greater commitment of people at work. Ineffective supervision is costly; disputes, excessive turnover, absence and so on. Well-trained, well-led supervision is the most effective way of ensuring good productivity.

A supervisor is the manager of his or her team and an integral part of the management structure. The supervisor's purpose will be most effectively carried out if they are: well selected, prepared, trained and developed, and the role clearly defined.

A profile of the ideal Supervisor

The supervisor is expected to perform a wide range of functions. How effectively will depend on many things: aptitude, knowledge, training, attitude and so on. The supervisor works at many levels; here we show the performance criteria of successful supervisors, as it looks to their managers, and to themselves:

The manager says that the supervisor:

- ✓ gets the work done
- ✓ keeps the costs down
- ✓ makes good decisions
- ✓ has good ideas
- ✓ uses initiative well
- ✓ is dependable, loyal and well-liked
- ✓ takes responsibility
- ✓ has few complaints from staff
- ✓ has few accidents
- ✓ keeps staff turnover down
- ✓ produces accurate output
- ✓ carries out orders
- ✓ does not short-circuit.

The supervisor says:

- ✓ my manager consults me
- ✓ he likes my ideas
- ✓ he gives me freedom
- ✓ he gives me more authority and responsibility
- ✓ my department rums smoothly
- ✓ there is a minimum of conflict
- ✓ my staff work well
- ✓ my staff are loyal
- ✓ my staff do not ask for transfers.

The major criteria can be summarised into six essential things a supervisor does:

> ✓ **makes good decisions**
> ✓ **motivates people to work well**
> ✓ **has control of the situation**
> ✓ **assumes responsibility**
> ✓ **treats everyone fairly**
> ✓ **inspires confidence.**

The Supervisor as leader

Any enterprise depends on maximising efficiency of resources available – financial, technical and human. The most important and difficult is people, this needs effective leadership. There is a constant demand for supervisors who are also effective leaders.

Too often people are made supervisors because they are good craftspeople, or made managers because they are good engineers, accountants or sales people. **But no training is given in management skills**. They frequently fail, or manage poorly. This is the 'Peter Principle' which states that 'a person is promoted to the level of his or her incompetence'.

A supervisor must have the technical competence to achieve the results required and also have the understanding and skills of leadership so as to get work done by others.

Traditional methods of motivation are becoming less effective, so the importance of the leader increases. Supervisors have to stand or fall by their own performance, ensuring that each person gives their best to the job. A supervisor is responsible and accountable for the subordinates' work, making full use of their strengths, abilities and qualities, and constantly trying to improve performance. This is the object of effective leadership. Most individuals react well to good leadership; it is important to them that their abilities be fully used. For the enterprise, it is essential that people are not wasted.

To get you thinking:

Frustration factors

Here are a number of factors which tend to frustrate you in your role as a supervisor. Rank these ideas from 1=high to 12=low.

Factors	Rank
1. Company policy	____
2. The activities of higher management	____
3. The activities or inefficiencies of other sections of your organisation	____
4. The paperwork and red tape in your organisation	____
5. Trade union and/or staff council activity	____
6. The fact that you have too much to do in too little time	____
7. Poor physical working conditions and/or lack of equipment in your section	____
8. Your own lack of technical knowledge and/or training	____
9. Your own ability to handle people and/or communicate	____
10. Your own lack of motivation and/or enthusiasm for your job	____
11. The fact that some or all of your staff are awkward, lazy, disruptive etc.	____
12. Poor quality/low standard of ability of staff. Please state below why this situation exists, e.g. low pay, shortage of applicants for vacancies, poor training facilities, poor selection, etc.	____

_____

_____

_____

_____

_____

Frustration factors – commentary

The frustration factors fall into three broad categories: (1) your bosses; (2) your people and (3) yourself.

Items 1, 2, 3, 4 and 7 can essentially be seen as factors outside of your control, and, insofar as they hamper you in doing your job, they are highly frustrating. You will probably have ranked one of these as your number 1, and very likely others as your 2 and 3. As far as Item 7 is concerned, does the safety aspect worry you?

Items 5, 11 and 12 relate to the people you work with. You will probably have ranked them from 5 to 9. They are irritations, but not totally out of your control; you can have some influence. At least you can say your bit in the Works Council and maybe motivate your staff a little. When thinking about Item 12 consider what it is that makes for the low quality of your staff. Is there anything you can do about any of these things that will lessen your frustration level. You have probably ranked this item quite high, maybe 5 or 6. It is certainly an important factor.

Items 6, 8, 9 and 10 of course concern you. And unless you are brutally honest with yourself, you have probably ranked most of them quite low, say from 9 to 12. Your own failures, in time management, motivational, communication and technical skills, frustrating though they are, are not your fault – or are they? You are probably right to rate them low down as frustration factors. But these problems are within your own hands to solve. Hopefully, as you read on through the rest of this book, you will gather some ideas which will help you sort out these areas of frustration.

3

Leadership

'Most of us would rather be led than managed.'
Field Marshall Lord Slim

As President Eisenhower put it 'Leadership is persuading people to want to do what we want them to do.' It is also influencing them in such a way that they will work together towards some goal they have come to find desirable.

Need for leadership

Every group needs a leader (factually or emotionally), but the success of the leader is determined by the reaction and behaviour of the group being led, and how the leader satisfies their perceptions of a good leader.

A manager should be a leader. Judgement is on results, not only of the individual but of the whole department. How those results are achieved will depend on how well the available resources – people, money, materials – are deployed and how well motivated the team has been to achieve the results. This is not a one-off exercise. The manager will continue to carry out the job, and must therefore be able to keep the team behind him or her. A leader will also be judged by success in solving problems that affect the whole group.

Characteristics of a good leader

- **Inner drive**
  Good leaders have a powerful urge that makes them want to get things done, to organise, to take responsibility.

- **Intelligence**
  They are often more intelligent than most. But they are not often 'superior' about it. They ensure that they can be readily understood by those working with them, and understand their difficulties. They are, therefore, good communicators.

- **Maturity and openness of mind**
  Good leaders are emotionally balanced; they will not be crushed by defeat or over-elated by success. They are aware of most of their own prejudices and hostilities and so can keep them to a minimum. They are never afraid that new ideas might threaten them or their status. Because their judgement is balanced, they can make confident decisions.

- **Attitude to people**
  A good leader knows that the job is done through people, and always tries to know them better. They approach problems more in terms of the people involved than of the technical difficulties. They always try to preserve and develop human dignity. They see themselves as the 'servant' of their subordinates, and hold themselves personally responsible for what they do and how they work. They are not afraid to be 'tough' with people when occasion demands it. But this toughness is for emergencies rather than as a disguise for lack of confidence.

Some 'golden rules' for good leadership:

Do:
- be fair – do not develop favourites
- be prepared to take the blame
- take responsibilities in your stride
- give sincere justifiable praise
- back up and support your team loyally
- develop a sense of loyalty to your company and team

Don't:
- make promises you can't keep
- take credit for someone else's good ideas
- pass the blame
- be afraid to make mistakes
- change – become 'big headed' or over concerned with status
- lose your 'cool' – control your temper under pressure
- criticise company policies and action in front of subordinates.

Types of authority

A leader must develop as much authority as possible, maintain that authority and use it effectively. Do not make the mistake of thinking that authority is something that arises solely from your title, your position in the organisation or your job description. There are different types of authority, which are relevant in industry or commerce.

Structural authority
Based on the position a person holds within the structure of an organisation, e.g. rank in the Army or job description and responsibility in industry.

The important thing for a leader to know is how to use the structural authority that you have. The golden rules are 'don't use it all unless you have to', be careful 'not to exceed the structural authority that you have', and 'ensure that the subordinates are in no doubt as to its extent and implications'.

Knowledge authority
Based on the knowledge, skill and experience of the individual. To maintain this authority a leader should:

　i) keep in touch with his subordinates and their work
　ii) keep up to date with technical developments and new ideas
　iii) go on relevant training courses.

There is often nothing wrong with a subordinate having more technical skill or knowledge than the supervisor. If this is the case do not pretend to have knowledge authority which you do not really have. If you decide that you need to increase such authority then ask questions of your subordinates and seniors and have some formal training.

Moral authority
Based on the integrity and 'goodness' of the individual. It is behaviour rather than knowledge or position which gives rise to moral authority. It is acquired from the respect your subordinates have for you. To increase your moral authority:

- ☑ keep your word
- ☑ give credit when due
- ☑ show respect for people and treat them as individuals
- ☑ be considerate
- ☑ treat your staff fairly but firmly and equally
- ☑ practice what you preach
- ☑ combine self-confidence with modesty
- ☑ be genuine, natural and relaxed.

Charismatic authority
Based on the personality and natural powers of leadership of the individual. Charisma is to a large extent 'born not made'. Some people are natural leaders and some are not. However, we should all make the most of what we have. This means appearing to your subordinates as confident in yourself and your decisions, an effective communicator, well turned out, cool under pressure, well organised, enthusiastic and

a source of strength and encouragement in times of trouble.

These are the four types of authority by means of which you can exert influence. A good leader will rarely, if ever, use structural authority to get things done. A poor leader will depend on structural authority which in turn will make him a worse leader still.

Leader versus Driver

Some people are leaders, with an innate sense of how to carry out their job. Some are drivers who may have all sorts of personality problems which are displayed in their attitudes and how they do their job. Here are some comparisons:

The Leader	The Driver
• Motivates by increasing satisfaction	• Motivates by fear through threats of decreasing satisfaction
• Trusts his subordinates	• Trusts no one
• Delegates authority whenever possible	• Always demonstrates their own authority
• Gives reasons for orders and instructions	• Expects orders to be obeyed blindly and without question
• Gives credit where due	• Takes credit him- herself
• Exercises power through people	• Exercises power over people
• Believes that most people want to do a good job if given the opportunity	• Believes that no one will do a good job unless forced to do so
• Sees subordinates as human beings, who can be trusted to put their hearts into the task	• Sees subordinates as replaceable production units who can only be persuaded by fear or by appeals to the lowest form of self-interest

Leadership

- Maintains a discipline that is contributory and a sign of subordinates' respect
- Inspires loyalty and initiative

- Maintains a discipline that is defensive and a sign of subordinates' fear
- Demands blind obedience

There are significant difference between the true leader and the taskmaster (driver). In the short term the driver may seem to be more successful, but will lose out to the real leader over the long run.

We will see, as we read on, that the motivational ideas that are covered later exactly describe the characteristics of the Leader and the Driver. Occasionally, if we are honest, a bit of a Driver is needed; but the effective supervisor will always strive to use real Leadership skills wherever possible.

Leadership and group management

Managing groups effectiveness and productivity involves the relation of the group's structure and dynamics to its' task performance. Every group operates in three interlocking areas:

- **Group task**

Most groups have some task to do, and exist mainly to carry out that task. Often they are so conscious of the need to get this task done that they forget the other areas – group maintenance and individual needs – which are operating simultaneously.

- **Group maintenance**

People working together on a task as a group, are also doing something to and with each other. A group is a constantly changing network of interactions and relationships. A group develops a keen awareness of itself as a group, and faces the need to maintain the relationships within it, if the task is to be done. Maintenance refers to what is happening to persons as the task is being carried out.

- **Individual needs**

Every individual brings a particular set of needs which affect the group and its task. It is here that we are most found wanting. Individual needs are frequently well hidden behind the task drive of the group, or behind usual behaviour patterns.

The group operates to balance these three areas and becomes more effective and mature. When one or more of these areas is neglected, the efficiency of the group is impaired and its growth slows down.

The task of the leader can easily be seen in a well-known simple model of three circles, one for each need. Make sure that these needs are satisfied by actions that either:

- help the group achieve its task
- maintain group togetherness
- satisfy needs of individual members.

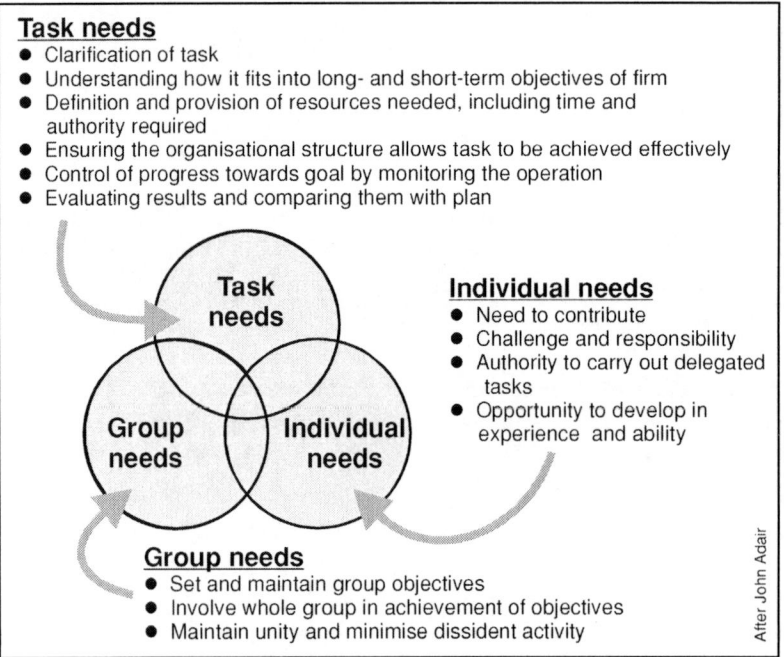

Figure 1 – Task, group and individual needs

In the model, the circles overlap. They are not isolated; actions by the leader in one area will have effects in one or both of the other areas. Thus, effort aimed at meeting the needs of the group, or the individual, derive from the need of the leader to achieve the task. Conversely, successful achievement of objectives is essential if the group is to be held together; or the individual is to be motivated to give his or her best effort to the job. Again, if the leader takes action to strengthen the team, it will make each individual more confident and the team more likely to succeed in its task.

For example, remove the group needs circle from the model. This will obviously create gaps in the other two. This is a clear signal that unless the leader actively satisfies the needs of the group, chances of achieving the required results in the long-term are doubtful. Similarly the group and individual circles may become exhausted, for instance after a period of hard pressure. The leader must take prompt action to revive them, and pay specific attention to these areas.

Leadership is a prime role for the supervisor. Whether wished for or not, it will be thrust upon them. The job title, the activity, the work demands it. It needs courage and determination to make this part of the job a success.

Here is a good statement that sums up leadership:

> *A leader is best*
> *When people scarcely know that he exists*
> *Not so good when they blindly obey and acclaim him,*
> *Worse when they despise him,*
> *Fail to honour people*
> *They fail to honour you.*
> *But of a good leader, who talks little,*
> *When his work is done, his aim fulfilled,*
> *They will all say, 'We did this ourselves'.*
>
> Lao Tzu (circa 500 B.C.)

To get you thinking:

Thinking about leadership

Here is a list of elements of the leader's role briefly stated. Try to decide how good/bad you are at each of them. Rank (1, 2, 3) your three strongest areas in the left hand column and your three weakest areas in the right hand column. For the purposes of this questionnaire, ignore factors outside your control, and concentrate on your own personal abilities.

Strongest	Leadership Element	Weakest
	HIRING the right people for the right jobs.	
	ORGANIZING the work of your team so that they work well together.	
	DIRECTING your staff by initial induction and training and target setting.	
	MOTIVATING them to give of their best.	
	CONTROLLING your team by giving them the right kind of supervision.	
	CORRECTING your staff when they go astray in either technical or disciplinary matters	
	ASSISTING those of your team who need either personal or technical help.	
	DEVELOPING your staff to make the most of their abilities and potential abilities.	
	DECISION MAKING so as to get the best possible decision in the available time.	
	CHANGING systems and procedures when necessary and overcoming resistance to change	
	INSPIRING your team when things are going badly	
	RETAINING those staff who are good performers	
	FIRING those staff who are bad performers.	

Leadership Quiz – Commentary

This is an interesting test of self-integrity. The idea of thinking about your strongest and weakest leadership characteristics is simply that – to get you thinking. We generally accept the things we do in our job, without any real analysis; it's something we do. But in relation to our leadership style, it is worth considering how well we do some things, how poorly we may do others.

To take just a few examples: some of us pull back from any degree of personal conflict, so we may not be very good at 'correcting', or 'controlling', or 'firing'. Some of us may be very good at 'organising', or 'directing', or even 'motivating', but have we got the right training and background knowledge to be good at 'hiring'?

Obviously the leadership elements mentioned need a great deal of amplification and we shall cover many of them in this book. But for now, just spend a little while pondering 'how am I doing?'. Maybe if you can identify strengths you will be able to build on them -'I am really good at 'assisting'; think about this; are you really assisting, or just doing it for them? Similarly, examine the whole list and be as self-critical as you can. Nobody else will know about it, unless you want them to. And the process might just make you a bit better as a leader.

4

Organisation and Planning

'Mix a little folly with your serious plans.'
                                                    Horace

Organising your team

A supervisor is in charge of other people. It is necessary to organise activity for maximum effectiveness. Here are some pointers for organising the team:

- ☑ Distribute the workload equally (or at least fairly). Allow adequate time for peaks and troughs.

- ☑ All sections of the team should work in harmony towards the group objective; avoid pulling in opposite directions: try to satisfy conflicting individual section goals.

- ☑ Organise for maximum flexibility, to enable the team to respond to change and to cope with the unforeseen things that do happen.

- ☑ Define the responsibilities, objectives, limits of authority and lines of communication of each section of the team very clearly. These should be known by the whole team.

- ☑ No person to report to more than one supervisor.

☑ Don't have too many subordinates reporting directly to the supervisor. (**Never** more than 15 – and that's too many!)

☑ Don't organise the team round one key individual.

Organisation charts show lines of structural authority and communication. They often show what the people involved think they ought to be. An organisation chart will not alter the way people work, but may help the supervisor identify weaknesses in the structure.

A supervisor must do more than point people in the right direction and see them on their way. Real supervision means making sure that they continue on the right track; that means planning for what has to be done and controlling the activity. Control comes from supervision and feedback of information.

Planning

Introduction
We start with an **Intention**, we wish to end with a **Result**. Planning is the bit in between.

> **Planning is a process of imagining future events; a synthesis of facts, assumptions and fantasies with the aid of logic, vision and judgement.**

Some people plan in precise detail, others in broad brush. Some think of the future using their past experience; others use abstract thought and apply knowledge learned in one situation to entirely different situations.

We are concerned with planning in a business context. The task is to produce practical profitable results, from plans which are usually a co-operative effort to prepare, and the work of a team to carry out.

Planning objectives
We cannot plan unless we have an **Objective**. 'Objective' can mean different things to different people. It can lead to wrong emphasis on

priorities, and thus management difficulties. Often, too much attention is given to **means** without the **ends** being clear. Planning starts with Objectives and ends with Results. If results are to work out as intended there must be a continuity of planning in between.

Generally people will produce the usual result by going through familiar routines without the need for much planning or control. If we want a different result we need detailed planning, re-education and tight control.

The importance of planning

To do anything, deliberate thinking ahead is a must. Unless one thinks far and widely enough ahead, actions will be often be a series of unrelated, ad hoc decisions and maybe pointless activity.

When many events have to relate to each other – as they always do in business – planning is essential. So the quality of results is determined by the quality of planning.

There must be a continuous arrangement of interrelated plans from where objectives start to where results happen. Broad intentions may be perfectly sound and clearly expressed, but beware of the gaps and wrong assumptions. Gaps in planning are the main cause of wasted business effort.

There is also the question of who should plan for what, and the time frame for the various management levels. For example, there is no point in supervisors planning a year ahead; that would be a waste of effort and a distraction from doing the job. But planning is not an isolated activity; it is interdependent at every level. Supervisors can only plan effectively if they are informed of the intentions of their managers, similarly they have to pass on their plans to their subordinates, so that their plans can work efficiently. The planning triangle illustrates these relationships.

Organisation and Planning

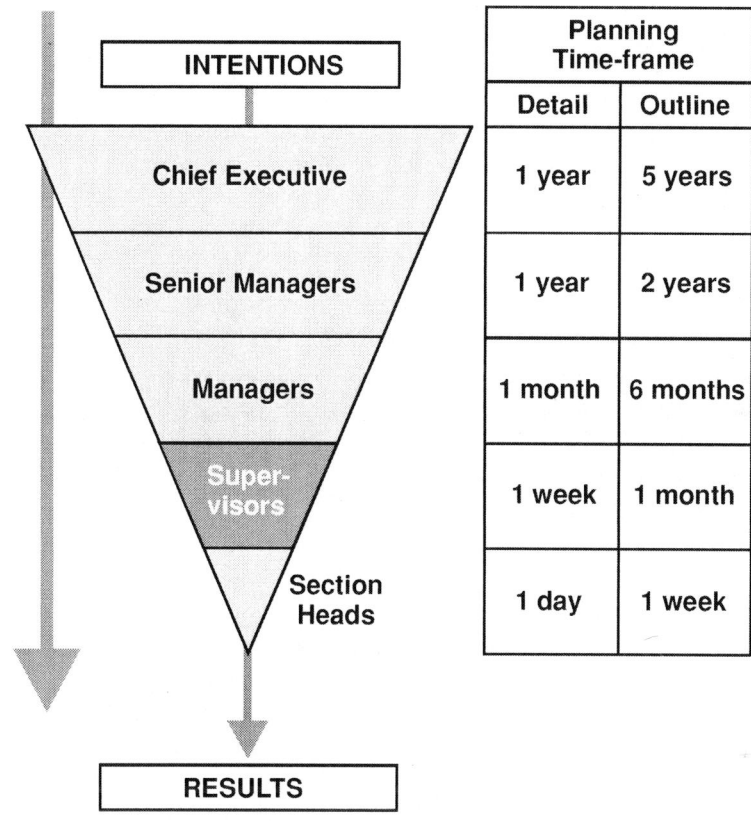

Figure 2 – The Planning Triangle

Planning for control

For successful results, plans must be sound and capable of control by management. Whether this is possible will depend on how plans are formulated. A plan must be designed to be enforceable; this requires clearly defined points at which control is exercised.

We may know that objectives are feasible, (somebody else has done it), but not how results will be achieved. It may be impractical therefore to try and plan in detail at too early a stage. This does not mean we should not plan at all; but the planning is of a different type; plan the approach rather than the details of execution. Go as far as possible with the available information at the start. This means clarifying objectives, deciding the approach and discovering how much one does not know! As more information becomes available, the plan advances another stage. Step by step, the total plan emerges; often over a long period and as the collective responsibility of many people.

In planning, it is very easy to lose sight of the purpose; to get side tracked by unimportant details. It is difficult to be objective and admit that personal beliefs may be wrong.

Keep asking these questions:

? What are we trying to do?
? How do we know this is true?

Planning involves many people. Unless they understand and agree with the objectives, they may work at cross-purposes. So it is worthwhile to spend time planning how planning is to be done. This will save people from solving the wrong problems and avoid wasted effort.

It is important to have people participate in plans that affect them. People's attitudes can make the difference between plans working out and not working properly. To get the best from each individual, responsibility and guidance have to be adjusted to individual needs. Find out what people's abilities are and make the level of planning appropriate for the people who will carry the plans out.

One final important point: people who are already familiar with change, react more favourably to further change than those with set habits. The amount of change and the time allowed for implementation has to be related to the past history of accepting new ideas. This should be taken into account in the overall planning process.

How to plan

There are many methods of planning, from super formal computerised models to simple back-of-an-envelope stuff. You will evolve your own method to suit your own needs. But there are a few constants which always need to be taken into the planning process:

- Set the objectives, and set the results. The objectives may already be specified and outside of your control, so your job is to get the results.

- Check resources available: people, equipment, space, logistics and, above all, the budget.

- Consider the time aspect: when do you start, what are the progress points, when do you have to deliver?

- Use some means of getting all your information down on paper (mind maps, Gantt chart, critical path diagram, scatter graphs – whatever suits you). If you can't see it all, you can't realistically work out how everything fits together and what comes first, and what follows, and so on.

- Once you have your data visible, in some form, you are beginning to get a plan.

- Check for feasibility – can this be done, with the resources, in the time.

- Put control points in to ensure that the plan is on track.

- Be ready to adjust the plan as necessary to maintain its viability; or even **abandon it if it is no longer functioning**. There is nothing more stupid in management than to press on with a plan that is no longer functioning.

To get you thinking:

Thinking about planning

We all know how to plan, most of us do it, consciously or unconsciously. If we are going shopping, we make a list – a rudimentary plan; if we are going on holiday, say by car, we plan the route, where we are going to stop each night – our objective – where we wish to get to eventually – our result. Of course it gets more complicated.

Think out a plan for yourself; imagine a work or personal scenario:

- What do we want to do?
  (State the objective.)

      _____

      _____

      _____

- What activities do we need to achieve the objective?
  (Put down a logical sequence of steps that have to be taken to get where you want to be.)

  1) _____
  2) _____
  3) _____
  4) _____
  5) _____

- Where will we get to?
  (What will the result be; state this.)

      _____

      _____

Organisation and Planning

- What will be the benefits from this process? (Try to evaluate the usefulness of this whole process.)

  _____
  _____
  _____
  _____
  _____

When you have done this, sit back and think a bit. The effort has cost you time, but has it saved you time in the long run? Have you been a bit confused as to what you were going to do? Is it clearer now? Does your plan now have a shape to it? The benefits of clear and logical thinking are enormous. Try to plan more often.

5

Controlling

'I don't think I've controlled events; but plainly events have controlled me.'
Abraham Lincoln

What is control?

Controlling is an essential part of the supervisor's job. But 'Control', when applied to people, can be an emotionally charged word. To the authoritarian supervisor, it implies the ability to command, dominate or manipulate people or events. To those being controlled the word control is not appealing. It is the way control is used in relation to people that causes difficulty.

One of the meanings of the word is to describe a natural relationship between cause and effect. It is in this sense that we are interested in control.

The principles of control relate to:

- man within himself – unconsciously (motivation)

- man within himself – consciously (self-control)

- **man controlling other people (supervision)**

- man controlling a machine (driving a car)

- a machine controlling itself (automatic pilot)
- a machine controlling other machines (automation).

The planning spectrum must be continuous from intentions to results. If results are to happen as intended, it is essential to build in some form of control. For control to be possible, there must be a plan in the first place. So, there are four basic conditions for anyone to do a job correctly and efficiently:

1. a plan
2. ability to carry it out
3. feedback (in time to enable action to be taken)
4. corrective action.

And there are six steps to controlling anything:

1. Identify the key factors to control.
2. Measure what is happening to the key factors.
3. Compare what is happening with the plan.
4. Find the cause of differences between the plan and what is actually happening.
5. Decide corrective action.
6. TAKE ACTION.

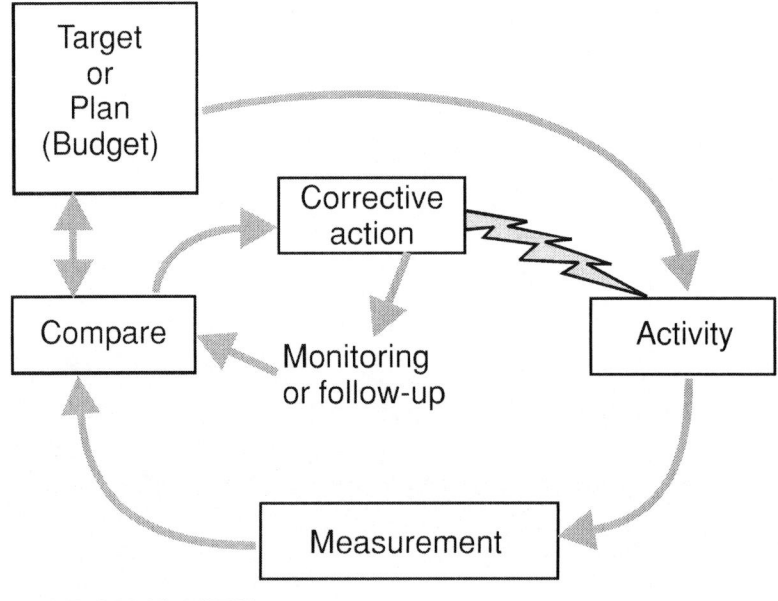

ACTION IS VITAL
WITHOUT ACTION THERE CAN BE NO CONTROL

Figure 3 – The control circle

The Control Cycle shows the sequence of events for any activity that is controlled to a plan. The essential element is corrective action. There is no point in knowing if something is going wrong if you don't do something about it!

Supervisory control

There is a double aspect to a supervisor's job:

- the logical, reasoning process of 'deciding what to do'
- the ability to handle people in order to 'get it done'.

Supervisory control depends on intellect for planning (including the design of control arrangements), and on emotion for getting people to carry out plans. The willingness to undertake any task depends on the relationship between the difficulty of the task and satisfaction we get from doing it. Satisfaction may be a sense of achievement in accomplishing something, controlling or power, or from financial rewards. To get satisfaction we have to be aware of the results of our work because motivation depends on feedback; it is important for people to know what progress they are making.

- Feedback is getting information about what is happening;
- Motivation depends on feedback.

Feedback can take the form of a verbal or written report, or we can go and take a look for ourselves. One of the disadvantages of written feedback is that it can involve a time lag. Poor communication by the sender may invalidate it. However, to be effective, a supervisor must have a system of checking on his team members.

Accountability

What supervisors employ people to do and what people themselves feel they are being paid to do, can be quite different.

The concept of accountability, which broadly covers the idea of responsibility, implies two questions:

- What makes people willing to be accountable? (Motivation)
- How should they account? (Control)

For a person to be willing to be accountable requires:

- knowing what is expected
- knowing what he or she is achieving
- having the knowledge, the authority and the means of sufficiently influencing the operations he is responsible for.

These are also the conditions for control. And, as we have seen, they create the conditions thatenable the supervisor to do an effective job.

To be held accountable, people must be in a position to control what they are accountable for. If someone is to be accountable, first make sure that authority matches responsibility. Be certain that the person knows what is expected. Clarification of these things is essential.

Accountability also includes the sense of rendering an account of your actions – admitting responsibility if things go wrong and accepting the applause if things go right. You cannot slide out of accountability with some lame excuse – it means that it is down to you.

Management by objectives

If people are to accept accountability for something, they cannot be truly satisfied until they have achieved the things they committed themselves to do; or until they have made an attempt they can be proud of. This enhances their self-esteem.

'Managing by Objectives' is making a plan, then controlling the work of putting the plan into practice, by measuring actual results.

When people are not used to having their results measured, it can worry them. There is a lot of difference between agreeing to a target being possible, and to feeling deeply committed to achieving it. To accept accountability for results, an individual must feel confident of achieving the results. The opportunity to demonstrate success is needed; also guidance in the job until there are mostly successes and few failures. We need to build confidence.

Supervision implies personal checking of someone's work; this is the most precise method of control. Some, or all, of direct personal supervision can be delegated. There is no one right amount of supervision for everybody. Some people work best with little supervision, others need a lot, few people need none at all. A supervisor has to make an individual assessment and use the right amount for each person.

The alternative to personal supervision is indirect feedback by time sheets, daily reports, weekly or monthly figures etc. The advantage of this is that everybody is providing the same amount of information. The disadvantage is that it is remote, but the reports etc. do provide the clue as to the different levels of checking needed.

Control systems

Control systems range from nothing on paper (all done in the head!) through paper-based systems to computer-based controls. For simple processes, we can remember what has to be done and then compare the results with our intentions, in our head. Often we make mistakes by relying too much on memory. If we realise that we are likely to forget, we can use a checklist as a basis for (some) control.

A checklist can be a simple paper list with items to be checked off or it can be a list on a board for all to see, e.g. a schedule of shifts or work to be carried out which can be checked off when completed. This gives us some (but not much) information. However, in some situations it may be sufficient. Don't over-elaborate!

Slightly more sophisticated paper-based reports use specifically designed forms which provide quite a lot of information. This, when accumulated over a period of time, will show trends which could be useful and give the management an idea of how production is going and how the supervisor is performing. Such 'after the event' controls give management useful data.

In any control system, speed and clarity are usually more important than great accuracy. Do not delay or confuse data with too much detail when a few prompt simple facts give the same result. The ideal is quick, low cost information sufficiently accurate to put the supervisor on track to the right decisions.

Presentation

- Data should invite action.
- Managers do not enjoy digging for meaning in a mass of figures.

- Highlight the abnormal: Management by exception.
- Some people understand graphs and diagrams more easily than figures.

Speed and intelligibility
There is no point in having information which cannot be understood or which arrives too late to do anything about.

Complexity

- Keep information to a minimum but ensure that it is key information.
- A maximum of seven items on one piece of paper is a good aim.

Frequency

- Match frequency to the possibility for taking action. For supervisors daily (or per shift), for middle management weekly or monthly, for top management monthly or quarterly are typical.

Integration

- In any system the control at each management level should summarise the results of the control at the lower level.
- Ensure that irrelevant information is eliminated when obsolete because of changed conditions.

Data collection and processing for any control system is obviously a suitable job for computerisation. But however the data is collected and processed, the answers always end up on somebody's desk. Control statements are the vital link between the system and people.

Controlling

To get you thinking:

Control checklist

Use this checklist to think critically about your control. Ensure that your control process is comprehensive. Tick the Yes/No boxes to get an overall picture of how it is going and what still needs to be done.

General	Yes	No
Have I clear objectives and plans for all my critical areas?	❑	❑
Do I remember how people resent control and act accordingly?	❑	❑
Do I control by involving others early and by keeping their commitment at all stages?	❑	❑
Am I measuring results in all critical areas?	❑	❑

How do you think you are doing?

    OK ❑   Could do better ❑

For each critical area

Am I measuring the right things?	❑	❑

What does data collection cost? What are the benefits? _____

Is my data accurate enough to lead to good decisions?	❑	❑
Is it too accurate for its purpose?	❑	❑
Do the figures look more accurate than they really are?	❑	❑

How do you think you are doing?

    OK ❑   Could do better ❑

Control statements

Does the data invite action?	❑	❑
Would graphical presentation be better?	❑	❑
Are trends clearly shown?	❑	❑

Do I have to dig into the control to decide on action? ❑ ❑

If yes, should I redesign the control? ❑ ❑

Does everyone concerned use and understand the control? ❑ ❑

Do I get a good measure of the important intangibles? ❑ ❑

Do I get my information on time to take effective corrective action? ❑ ❑

If not, would less accurate information presented sooner be better? ❑ ❑

How do you think you are doing?

OK ❑   Could do better ❑

Control checklist – commentary

Each section asks how you are doing. Try to be as objective as you can about this. If you have ticked over half the YESs in each section, it would be fair to say you are doing OK Anything less and you 'could do better'.

Control is a vital part of the supervisor's job, but it often slips. There are too many other 'more important' things happening.

You will, of course, have observed that all the questions are loaded in some way. It will be very difficult, if you are honest with yourself, to say Yes firmly to many of them. There is probably a grey area between Yes and No, which would be more comfortable. Also each question implies that you have to think through each aspect of your work and make decisions. For example, in the first question: do you have clear objectives? Have you got them written down, quantified, and who else knows? Or: what are your critical areas? Have you defined them, discussed them with your boss, your staff; what would be the consequences of failing in these areas?

There is a lot more in this checklist than appears at first sight! How are you doing?

6

Problem Solving

'He had acquired a flourish of his arm in clearing the world of its' most difficult problems – by sweeping them behind him.'
Charles Dickens

Introduction

One of the most important activities in which the supervisor is involved is problem solving. When problems, of whatever nature, arise, the supervisor will often be the closest to them, knowing the background and the underlying causes. Thus, problem identification and analysis of the symptoms that are occurring fall in the supervisor's area of responsibility. This is an unenviable but inevitable task; if problems are holding up the workflow, then the supervisor cannot fulfil the main objective of the job – to get things done. That being so, the problem needs to be solved in the most rational, time and cost effective way possible.

It is best to tackle the problem-solving task in a logical way; this involves an initial analysis of the background to the problem. Often, an understanding of what the problem is about puts you on the track of a reasonable solution. We can then identify the real problem, which symptoms conceal. We may deal with symptoms but sooner or later the problem will come up again. So it is vital to identify what the problem really is.

Having done this we can now attempt a solution to the problem, using a variety of techniques. Something which is often forgotten in the problem solving process is the final stage. This is evaluating to see if the solution is working and monitoring to ensure that it continues to work satisfactorily.

All this is a time consuming and onerous responsibility for the supervisor, but one which is an essential part of the job. A good problem-solving supervisor gets things done without too much fuss!

How to define and handle problems – a six-step process

1. **Define the problem**
   There are two kinds of problems: 'what' problems that require you to determine the precise cause, and 'how' problems that focus on how you are going to solve the problem, when the cause is known. It may be better to deal with most problems as 'what', until you are absolutely certain of the cause. We often tackle the symptoms of a problem rather than the real issue, because we assume we know the cause when in fact we don't. The real problem is not always apparent. For instance, complaints about salaries often conceal a real problem, such as a boring job.

2. **Gather the information**
   Gather everything: at this stage do not differentiate between facts and opinions. Then interpret the information; sift facts from opinions and select information which is relevant to the problem. At this point you may find that you have defined the wrong problem! Go back to Step One and start again.

3. **Develop solutions**
   Try to develop several solutions. Don't worry at this stage about how feasible a solution is. Look for as many solutions as possible from which you can choose the best.

4. **Select the best practical solution**
   Note the word 'practical'. If you can, pre-test your better solutions to identify the best. Run small pilot tests. In the end, this can save you considerable time and money. Otherwise, you may have to

analyse each of your solutions to determine which has the highest chance of succeeding and go with that, making changes and corrections as needed.

In theory, one solution might be ideal but not be economically practical at this stage. For example: if the office is overheating, a move to an air-conditioned building might be the ideal solution; a more practical one is to install fans.

5. **Put the solution into operation**
Now try your best practical solution. Carefully plan its introduction; decide what needs to be done, write these steps down, then begin. If working as a team, and assignments can be delegated, do so.

6. **Evaluate and monitor the effectiveness of the solution**
An important stage, which is frequently omitted. Make sure your solution is working. Have a plan for contingencies. This will help successful resolution of problems that happen later on. If there are problems, solve them by going through this 6-step process again.

An important tool to assist problem solving

Cause and effect diagrams (Ishikawa analysis)

This can be used to identify the cause of a problem or get better sense of a situation. The final diagram resembles a fishbone, so the technique is sometimes also called fishbone analysis. First, carefully define the problem, then work to identify likely causes of the problem. Then find the major causes. Once you have this information, try to connect all the causes back to the general problem visually. The box at the centre right represents the problem. The heavy centre line represents the main spine of the problem and the other bones represent the contributory causes. The main categories of most business problems are:

- Manpower
- Materials
- Methods
- Machinery
- Management
- Money

and these may often be used for the six boxes. Or use other main category headings where appropriate.

Draw lines to show relationships between causes and effects. As more lines are drawn, additional causes are traced to these problems. In searching for causes, you ultimately come to the root cause of the problem, the one you need to tackle before the others. The contribution other people make to the Cause and Effect diagram will give you deeper insight into the problem and improve your ability to communicate your solution.

This technique can be helpful in general problem solving. There are many others, but they tend to be complex and related to specific industrial or construction problems and so may not be relevant for our purposes.

Problem Solving

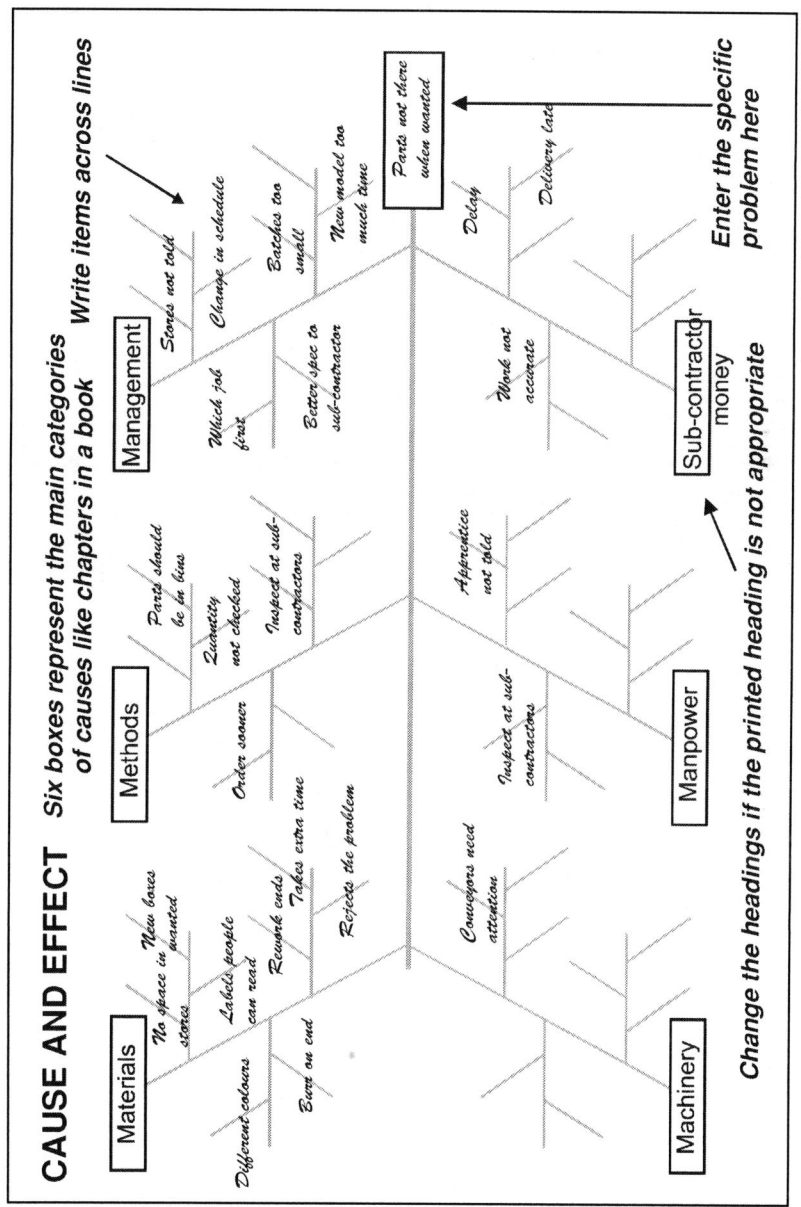

Figure 4 – Cause and affect

Problem solving ideas

This section gathers together a wide range of problem solving ideas, hints and tips that you can put into operation and get good results. We are primarily dealing with people centred problems, rather than technical matters. These can often be solved with a twist of a spanner, or a bang with a hammer. People, however, need gentler, more subtle treatment!

1. Dealing with difficult people
These tactics may help you cope with people who are difficult to deal with:

- **Kill with kindness.** Treat everyone well, no matter how people treat you. Be direct – but likeable and polite. It is difficult to treat a thoughtful person thoughtlessly.

- Listen, don't interrupt, then respond. Allow the difficult person to express their feelings fully. Acknowledge your awareness of the situation, describe what you see and hear, reveal what you think and feel, say what you want.

    Tip: Don't judge ('You shouldn't be that way') or generalise ('You always do that').

- Don't take a position – deal with a need. Find out what motivates the person, so that you can offer alternative ways of solving the problem. It is probable that the difficult person confronting you has simply adopted the most obvious solution. Move from what the person wants to why the person wants it.

- Accept blame. More often than not, you have played some role in bringing about the behaviour that others subject you to. Admit your fault quickly and emphatically. Whenever you shoulder your share of the blame, others are more likely to own up to theirs.

    Tip: Sometimes you can encourage the other person to co-operate by claiming more responsibility than you deserve.

Problem Solving

2. Settling disagreements

You may get into arguments where you and another person have developed rigid viewpoints. Your comments to each other become increasingly bitter until all progress stops. In most cases the basic problem is a breakdown in communication.

> Tip: Try this technique: Stop the discussion. Ask the other person to agree to a new ground rule for both of you:
> Neither will be allowed to speak up or to state their side of the argument until each has stated the opponent's ideas and attitudes to the other's complete satisfaction. In this way you are forced to think like your opponent and see their point of view.

3. Crisis and bad-news guidelines

Make sure your staff know how and when to let you know if things go wrong. Make it absolutely clear that you will NOT shoot the messenger. Offer them these guidelines:

- Report the problem promptly. Tell me right away; this will allow me to solve the problem before it gets worse.

- Give me only the necessary facts. Overstating the problem could make it look worse than it is. Think it through before you report and be ready to explain exactly what happened.

- Use tact. Don't say something like 'This is a terrible situation'. Instead say 'Here's something I thought you should know about'.

- Offer a solution. Don't just tell me we've got a problem. Recommend a way to correct a mistake or an error in judgement, and explain how you'll prevent it from happening again.

- Don't deliver only bad news. Pass along the good news also. That way, when you do have bad news, I'll take it better and your suggestions for improvement will have more impact.

4. How to make difficult decisions
If you have a difficult decision to make here are some suggestions:

- Accept that you can't control the outcome of a decision. All you can do is influence the decision-making process.

- Identify your needs and wants. Put them down on paper – even if they are contradictory. Writing things down helps to see a logical pattern in a problem.

- Rank the things you want and need. If you spot contradictory needs, ask yourself 'Which would I choose?

- Gather all the information necessary to make the decision. Look at alternatives, consequences, advantages and disadvantages. Do not let your emotions interfere with this process. Be as objective as possible.

- Determine how much of a risk you are willing to take. Consider these strategies.
  - ❖ Choose the safest alternative – one that can't fail.
  - ❖ Pick the option with the best odds for success.
  - ❖ Select the alternative with the most desirable outcome – despite the risk.

- Cut out any option that might present a loss you will not be able to accept – despite high odds for its success.

- Think out how you would deal with negative consequences.

5. Dealing with interrupters
Some people do not realise they are being disrespectful, cutting into your time, or disturbing your thought process when you are busy. That means you have to tell them. Establish clear guidelines, for the times when you cannot be interrupted.

Problem Solving

Some of the following ideas may be helpful. They are mainly Time Management techniques:

- Designate specific times for interruptions and other times for no interruptions. Put a sign on your door that you will be 'available after 10:30'. Or move your work to a conference room or library.

- Arrange with your boss and your staff times when you can generally get together without interruptions.

- When you have something to discuss, meet in the colleague's office. Then you can get up and leave when you feel the conversation is over. It is more difficult to get the colleague to leave your office.

- In making a presentation, avoid long-winded comments before you get to the point. Make your point before you explain it. Keep your remarks as brief as possible. If people interrupt, ask them to hold their comments until you have finished.

- Learn to tell people that you cannot talk now as you are working on something that must be done immediately.

- If someone interrupts say: 'I'd like to respond to that, but first, let me finish the point I was making'.

Problem solving needs a clear head. The supervisor is often involved in problem solving in crisis situations. This is inevitable. It is unlikely that the supervisor will have the luxury of sufficient time to go through or use the problem solving process that we have outlined. The main thing is not to panic, and try to put the first few points of the six-step process into action. This will have a calming effect and bring a useful result, which is what is wanted.

To get you thinking:

To help you think about problem solving

As an intellectual exercise, try using the Ishikawa analysis system to get to grips with some problem that you have, (although it is best used in groups).

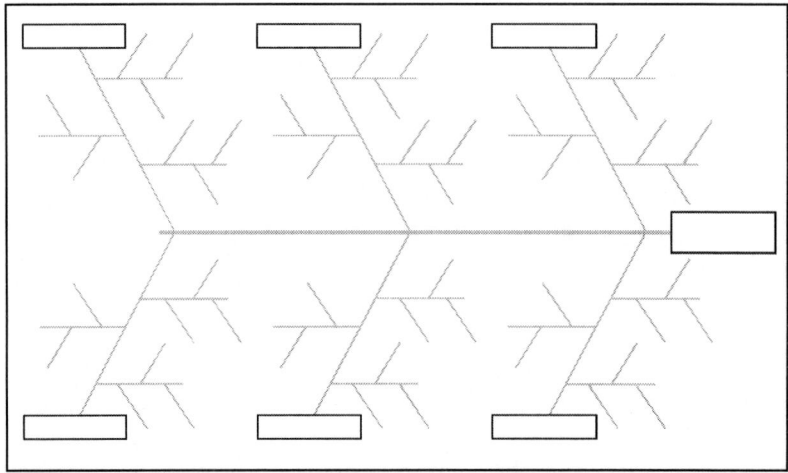

Draw out an Ishikawa diagram on a largish sheet of paper. Enter your problem and the main factors as you perceive them. Draw fishbones and put down all the facts or bits of information along the relevant bones.

What you will eventually have is a structured picture of your problem. You will not have a solution, but along the way you will have done a lot of thinking about it, that hopefully will have brought the problem into focus. This, again hopefully, will develop a sensible set of solutions out of which you can select the most appropriate and likely to succeed.

This is a time consuming process, and you can't really use it in an emergency. But it is certainly a helpful way of thinking around a problem.

7

Time Management

'I wasted time, and now time doth waste me.'
William Shakespeare

Managing your time

Some supervisors always seem to have enough time; why do they never seem to be too busy, no matter how many responsibilities they assume? The answer is – they manage their time effectively and efficiently. They recognise that all tasks do not have the same importance and give their most important responsibilities the most attention.

Peter Drucker says 'Some business people tend to confuse efficiency with effectiveness. Effectiveness is doing the right things; efficiency is doing things right.' He says 'There is nothing so useless as a supervisor doing, with great efficiency, what he should not have done at all.'

So we need to ask ourselves:

'Are we spending our time on our most important responsibilities? Do we clearly understand the difference between effectiveness and efficiency?'

Some Time Management principles

The most valuable thing we have is our time. We all have the same amount; when it's gone we cannot get any more. To be an effective supervisor we have to practice excellent time management. Some key principles are:

- **Anticipation.** Anticipatory action is generally more effective than remedial action. A stitch in time save nine. Avoid surprise by expecting the unexpected and planning for it. Assume if anything can go wrong, it will.

- **Planning.** We have already talked a lot about planning and you will have seen that the great majority of problems arise from action without thought. Every hour spent in effective planning saves three to four in execution, and achieves better results. By failing to plan you are planning to fail.

- **Objectives.** Effective results are achieved through purposeful pursuit of planned objectives. This is the fundamental concept of management-by-objectives.

- **Priority.** Time available should be budgeted to allocated tasks in ordered sequence of priority. Otherwise supervisors tend to spend time in amounts inversely related to the importance of their tasks.

- **Unrealistic time estimates.** Supervisors tend to take an optimistic view of the time a task will take them to complete. They also tend to hope that others will be able to complete their tasks sooner than is likely. Supervisors frequently accept, and expect from others, unrealistic time estimates.

- **Tyranny of the urgent.** Supervisors live in constant tension between the urgent and the important. The urgent tasks call for instant action and drive out the important from our consciousness. Supervisors are tyrannised by the urgent and respond unwittingly to the endless pressures of the moment. They thus neglect the long-term consequences of more important but less demanding tasks left undone.

- **Selective neglect/limited response.** Response to problems and demands should be realistic and limited to the needs of the situation. Many problems if left alone go away. By selectively ignoring those problems which tend to resolve themselves, much time and effort can be conserved for more useful pursuits.

- **Work expansion.** Work tends to expand to fill the time available. You will tend to fill up 'spare' time with trivia.

The Pareto principle

Some familiar examples illustrate a time management principle which applies to a wide range of human situations.

- A couple, sitting down to work out a family budget, find that nearly half their net income is spend on just two items – rent (or paying off the mortgage) and food.

- A salesman, planning next week's calls, finds that not all of his customers buy the same amount from him. Some place large orders, some small. In fact a small proportion of his customers account for a large proportion of his sales.

- An insurance company finds that the under-25 age group, although a small proportion of the total number of drivers, are involved in a much greater proportion of the total number of accidents.

This principle, known as Pareto's Principle after an Italian economist who first established the principle in the 1890s, says quite simply that:-

'A few causes account for most of the effect'.

(In more detail, the principle states that: 'In any series of events to be controlled, a selected small fraction in terms of number of elements, always accounts for a large fraction, in terms of effect.')

This principle applies in management.
Examples:-

- **Stocks**   20% (say) of all the items in a store account for 80% of the value.

- **Personnel**   a small percentage of employees account for most of the problems.

- **Quality**   a few of all the possible faults account for most of the rejects.

Pareto's Principle is really a trick to save work. It has a number of important implications for all supervisors.

1. In any situation where there are a number of factors, separate the VITAL FEW from the TRIVIAL MANY.

2. Don't give equal weight to all factors; find the VITAL FEW and give them VIP treatment. This is important for time management also. Concentrate on the vital few, don't waste time on chasing after trivia.

3. When gathering the information needed to solve a problem, note that most of the answers will come from a small amount of information (providing it is the right information on the right key points).

4. The right information is a question of quality rather than quantity.

5. Sheer volume of data rarely provides its own information automatically.

Whenever you are in a situation where:

- you have too much to do in the time available ... or ...

- you are wondering what can safely be delegated to subordinates,

REMEMBER PARETO! Find out what is most important and give that your serious attention.

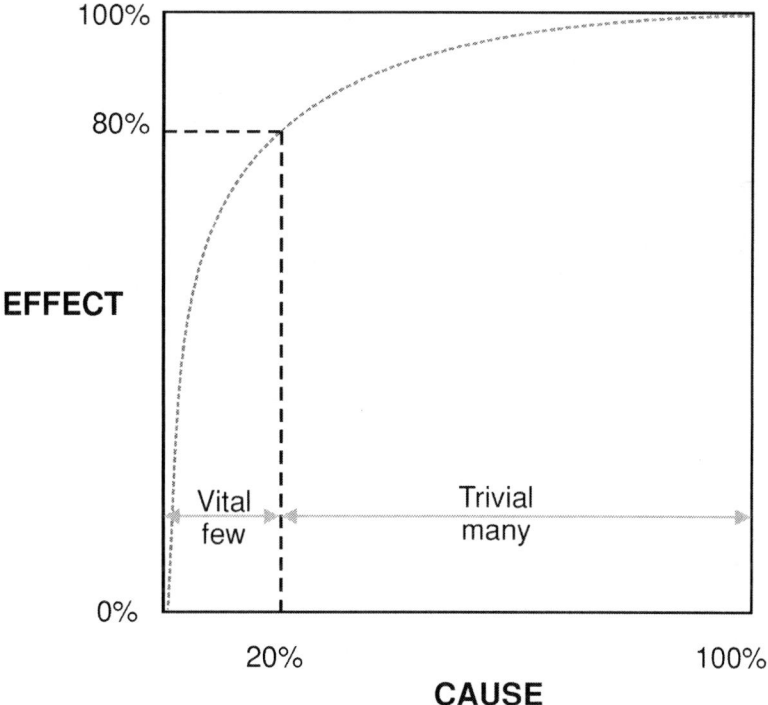

The Pareto Principle -
a few causes account for most of the effect

Figure 5 – The Pareto principle

Very few people use time as effectively as they could. We all waste time; we fritter it away, sometimes deliberately, most without noticing that we do. We kid ourselves that we are doing something useful with our time – then wonder why there is so much left to do at the end of the day. It's a puzzle as to where it all goes; some of the main time wasting categories are shown in the figure below.

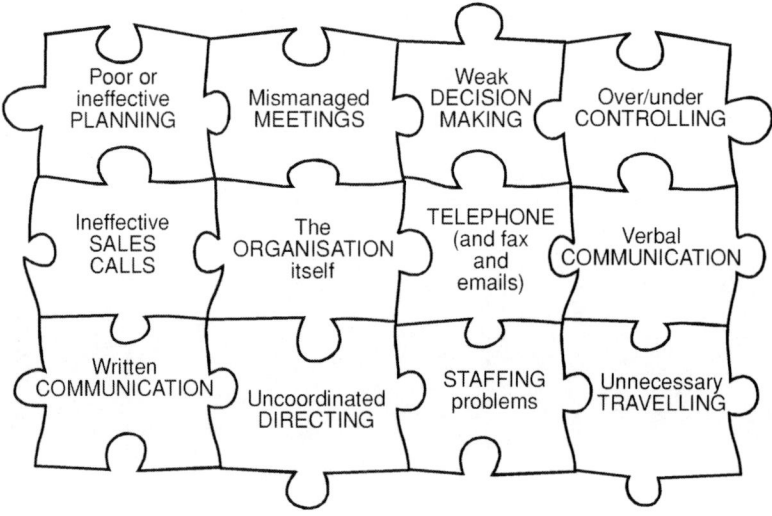

Figure 6 – The Time-waster Puzzle

Here are some of the time wasters that make up these headings. But be warned – the list is not exhaustive – you will be able to think of plenty more time wasters!

Planning – the most important function of management is plagued by these time wasters:

- lack of objectives
- no daily/weekly plan
- shifting priorities
- leaving tasks unfinished
- attempting too much
- unrealistic time estimates
- insufficient (or no) administrative assistance

Time Management

- lack of background information
- no self-imposed deadlines.

Meetings – are sometimes needed, but their effectiveness is often ruined by these time wasters:

- lack of preparation
- no agenda
- wrong people attending
- unscheduled meetings
- lack of procedures
- weak chairmanship
- domination by a single member
- difficult people.

Communication – telephone, written (letters, faxes, e-mails):

- interruptions by phone
- lack of preparation
- lack of structure
- unclear communication
- poor writing
- not listening
- excessive socialising
- incomplete information.

Sales Calls:

- procrastination
- seeing the wrong person
- lack of empathy
- overselling
- insufficient knowledge of product
- lack of research on the prospect.

Travelling:

- poor journey planning
- unnecessary journeys
- poor maintenance of equipment.

Administration

- lack of delegation
- no/poor filing systems
- badly kept records
- shuffling paper.

Uncoordinated directing:

- ineffective delegation
- 'Better do it myself'
- over-involvement in routine details
- not managing conflict
- not managing change
- no teamwork
- inability to say 'no'.

Staffing problems:

- over or under staffed
- personnel with problems
- untrained staff
- uncooperative, de-motivated staff.

Over/under controlling:

- overlooking poor performance
- mistakes
- ineffective performance
- over-control

- abdication of responsibility
- no standards
- no progress reports.

Weak decision making:

- snap decisions
- decision by committee (i.e. delay)
- procrastination
- wanting all the facts
- having too few facts.

We are all familiar with most of these timewasters. We have experience of them, indeed we actively indulge in many of them! If, in our daily work, we could get rid of a lot of these activities, we would be so much more effective – we would all have more disposable time. We could also achieve a better work/life balance and do some of the things in our personal life that we now neglect.

To get you thinking:

Do you have time management problems?

This short questionnaire will give you a quick overview of where you think you might have some time management problems. Quickly tick 'a problem' or 'not a problem'. Then do your scoring – but DON'T read the scoring before you have completed the quiz. This is for your eyes only; so there is no point in kidding yourself. Do the quiz honestly and you will gain some valuable self-knowledge.

	A problem for me	Not a problem for me
Procrastination		
Lack of organization		
Misplaced items		
Interruptions		
Waiting for information		
Attempting to do too much		
Unnecessary correspondence		
Meetings without goals		
Inability to say 'no'		
Difficulty listening		
Unclear objectives		
Socializing		
Ineffective delegation		
Confused choice of priorities		
Unrealistic time frame		
Negative attitudes		
Poor communication		
Other people's mistakes		
Understaffing		
Lack of feedback		

Time Management

Changing priorities		
Perfectionism		
Handling paperwork		
Too many goals		
Conflicting deadlines		
Too many appointments		

Scoring:

Each tick (✓) counts 1 point.

Count the number of responses in the 'A problem for me' column. If you've scored:

15 OR MORE   Danger! Ineffective time management – in your job and within your organisation – is seriously jeopardising your ability to succeed and reach your goals. You are a prime candidate for over-stress and job burnout. You need to do a LOT of work on time management skills.

8 TO 15   You will be unable to meet your goals and adhere to your high standards without improvement to your current organisational skills. But you can prevent an unmanageable situation from developing!

LESS THAN 8   You practice good time management skills. But you can become even more effective, productive and successful.

Managing your time effectively is the key to successful supervision. Some of the items in this quiz may not apply to you. Others could be a severe problem. Go through your 'problems' again. Try to assess how bad they are and how they could be affecting your work. Even if some of the 'problems' are beyond your control, you may, nevertheless, be able to make some improvements if you are aware of the problem – and every little helps!

8

Time Budgeting

'To choose time is to save time.'
Francis Bacon

Time Management is always topical. During downturns organisations cut back on investments, management and staffing levels. This means that the productivity of remaining staff is critical for survival. After cutback programmes, supervisors particularly, have greatly increased workloads – and time management problems.

But in times of business growth, organisations increase their investment and changes in organisation structures often take place. This too creates increased workloads and time management problems.

Business life is constantly changing, and it is speeding up. There are important new time management needs:

- Product life and development cycles are now a lot shorter. Being quicker to the market place gains competitive edge.

- Project management is now more complicated, on tighter deadlines and involves more people. Without good time management, project management falters.

- Investment payback cycles are shorter. A quick and high return is demanded.

- People management is now the concern of all managers. To be a good supervisor, you must be a good time manager: have time to listen, involve, communicate, direct and praise staff.

Time Budgeting

- Management moves much more. Travel and liaising with clients and suppliers all lead to time wastage!

- Quality of service is the key to success. This needs time to plan, think and respond.

- Work-related stress is a modern epidemic. Much stress is due to work and time pressures and relationships. Stress factors reduce with effective time management.

All these elements affect a supervisor's performance, Only about 40-50 percent of time is spent doing the things that are most important in the job. But a few changes to working style can produce a consistent increase in performance and save a lot of wasted time. This can be achieved using the Time Budgeting System (TBS).

TBS is a work method that focuses energy, skill and commitment on achieving high quality, top priority work. It is self-management for higher achievement. Self-management is concerned with developing a management style that focuses on important work and managing people effectively.

Key action points of the Time Budgeting System

- Say yes with enthusiasm to work.
- Say NO! effectively, if saying yes could seriously effect the completion of high priority work.
- Identify and concentrate on important work first.
- Control procrastination, the real enemy of self-management.
- Control stress: identify, confront and respond to the source of stress.
- Approach work in a positive and flexible way and know exactly what is needed to be achieved in the job.
- Schedule known and important work ahead. ❈
- Plan the time needed for thinking, and that needed for planned activity.
- Identify priorities ahead. ❈

- Control the diary or work schedule. Make sure time is available for known and important work. ❀
- Plan and control meetings. Emphasise action.
- Plan and brief work to be delegated with care. Follow up on these tasks.
- Develop teams of people by an emphasis on priorities, direction, involvement and harmony. Keep the team focused on success.
- Work effectively with secretarial and administrative staff.
- Be ruthless and quick with business reading, business writing, paperwork and routine work.

 ❀ **The Three Vital Points**

The time budget – an important time management technique

Reserve blocks of time ahead. Secure space in the diary/work schedule for known, important work that is due. For example, budget time – ensure that there is sufficient time to do it properly. Don't allow other current items to chip away at this reserve time. Reserve ahead in monthly blocks, but don't extend more than, say, three months ahead. Remember only reserve for known commitments, even though the exact task may not yet be clear, otherwise you are indulging in contingency fantasies.

Whatever the tasks, give them priority above all others; keep the time budget firm so as to reserve time in which to accomplish them. In practical terms, this guides supervisors to establish a work pattern that gives priority to the most important work (Pareto!). Keep tight control over the scheduling of meetings and appointments; at the same time reserve blocks of TBS time in which to do priority work, even when the precise nature of this work may not be known.

Supervisors will learn to reverse the tendency to 'fit in' their most important work around meetings and business appointments. By reserving in advance the time to complete important tasks, they then tackle them at the appointed time.

To make this happen, we need a 'critical mass' of people within the organisation, who all speak and practise the same 'common language' of effective time management. The TBS method helps to make this possible.

Projects and time management

Any supervisor will be involved in projects. These may be one-off, very time consuming and 'urgent'. Or they may be ongoing, not of major importance, but which continually use more time than they are worth. It is essential to control time usage on projects.

1. Establish goals and objectives for the project. Analyse and write out the three main constraints:
   - Time constraint – what are the deadlines?
   - Budget constraint – What are the resources (monetary, people, equipment).
   - Performance criteria – What are the quality specifications?

2. With your team, brainstorm all the necessary tasks that must be completed within the project. Group the tasks together into project 'chunks'.

3. Apply the three constraints to each task:
   - What is the estimated task duration?
   - What are the objectives and specifications for the task?
   - What is the budget for the task?

4. Determine the people to whom various tasks or 'chunks' of tasks can be delegated.

5. Determine the general order in which the tasks or 'chunks' of tasks must be completed. Look for tasks that cannot be performed

until another task is completed (dependant task). Also, look for tasks that can be completed simultaneously in order to save time (parallel tasks). Identify the critical path.

6. Create a bar chart for all of the tasks. Rewrite them in approximate chronological order down the left side of a sheet of graph paper. Write time increments across the top. Draw lines next to each task to correspond to the estimated time for the task and time increments. Plot dependent and parallel tasks also. Here is a simple example.

	Newsletter production							
Time	Task	Mar 5	Mar 12	Mar 19	Mar 26	Apl 2	Apl 9	Apl 16
1.5w	Research lead							
3wk	Sell ads							
2wk	Research others							
3wk	Write articles							
3wk	Design ads							
2wk	Full layout							

Figure 7 – A bar chart

7. With your team, brainstorm as many potential problems as possible. Develop contingency plans to keep the project within time, budget and specification constraints. Build in some, but not excessive, contingency time (say between 5-10%).

Hints on self organisation

To be an effective time manager, you really need to be organised, and organisation means self-discipline. This is hard! The following ideas expand on the TBS, and also rely very much on practicing the Pareto principle firmly.

- Make a 'To Do' list daily. Categorise tasks into:

    ❖ **Urgent**
    ❖ **Important**

Then prioritise.

- Be realistic – you can only do so much in one day. If you have tasks left over, carry them forward, re-prioritise. If this has happened more than three times – chuck them out – they don't need doing!

- Do not fill every minute with activities – allow for the unexpected. Review your list frequently and reorganise as needed.

- Before doing each task ask:
    'Why me?'
    'Can someone else do this?'

- Group related activities together to concentrate your efforts.

- Work on key tasks every day – focus on results, not urgency.

- Think ahead constantly. Don't neglect tasks you don't like so they eventually become urgent (and therefore a crisis).

Action meetings

Action meetings are great timesavers. They can replace general meeting (or information gatherings) already being held to discuss the same subjects, and are appropriate at all levels of management.

Action meetings are convened by a supervisor, for the people accountable to them. Thus the supervisor will meet with the foreman, charge hands, and so on.

The purpose of an action meeting is to:

- ❖ identify a problem
- ❖ decide on action
- ❖ by whom
- ❖ by when.

Action meetings should be informal and are important and useful. Here are some requirements for success.

1. Procedure

- The supervisor acts as chairman and receives the control reports for the department.

- The chairman should know the facts behind the control results. For the meeting to be a success good briefing is essential.

- The meetings should be strictly confined to getting the facts and making decisions. Involved discussions of detail should be done elsewhere. Any counselling of individuals which may be necessary should also be done elsewhere.

- The agenda also forms the minutes, and is in the form of an Action Statement. This means a minimum of work as all the information is on the same piece of paper.

- The first subjects to be considered at any meeting are those overdue from previous meetings. By this automatic follow-up, outstanding items get priority attention.

- Meetings should be short, decisive and to the point. They may even be held standing up.

No	Item	Date raised	Acton agreed	by whom	by when	Remarks

Action Statement
Date
Department
Present: _____ (Chair) _____

Figure 8 – Action statement

2. Effectiveness and success criteria

The effectiveness of Action Meetings depends very much on the supervisor's competence. They have to learn how to conduct them. Their success determines the usefulness of the management control system.

The supervisor, if taking the chair, should follow basic rules.

- **Be positive** – encourage suggestions for improvement (and listen to them!).

- **Do not hold post mortems.** (We can learn valuable lessons from the past, and do better in the future. But don't overdo it.) Action Meetings are not for allotting blame.

- **Be encouraging and interested** about the situation. But don't use pressure and give offence.

- **Never ridicule members.**

- **Conduct any disciplining away from the meeting.** (By careful questioning, the chairman may get a team member to admit mistakes to their colleagues.)

Other areas of Action Meeting chairmanship are similar to chairing any meeting and include:

- the ability to keep the meeting to the point
- the ability to persuade the meeting to the chairman's viewpoint, ... but ...
- the chair must be flexible in accepting the other points of view
- the ability to get sound decisions made
- the ability to get people to commit themselves to take action
- the ability to instil a sense of purpose, or even urgency, into discussions.

The main advantage of Action Meetings is their immediacy. If a problem arises, a quick creative solution can be found, and monitored. Action Meetings should be ad-hoc, as and when needed. They are one of the most effective ways of solving problems and not wasting time. The supervisor's competence is greatly enhanced by being able to conduct effective Action Meetings. It is a technique that can and should be learned.

Time Budgeting

To get you thinking:

What makes a good time manager?

'Managing Time' first of all means managing oneself.

Below are listed a number of ways in which you can judge how well a supervisor uses time.

1. Read them through, then choose three which, in your opinion, are the most important standards for judging whether a supervisor manages time well. Rank the three you have chose 1st, 2nd and 3rd.
2. Read through the list again. Do you think these are valid statements on which to judge a person's time management performance? Tick YES or NO for each statement
3. If you tick NO, give a short reason why in the space provided.

Rank		Yes	No
_____	1. is always busy	☐	☐
_____	2. takes work home	☐	☐
_____	3. can always get away promptly from the office	☐	☐
_____	4. subordinates work harder than he/she does	☐	☐
_____	5. gets the desired results in the available time	☐	☐
_____	6. does not waste other people's time	☐	☐
_____	7. is always ready to help	☐	☐
_____	8. makes it difficult for other people to interrupt him	☐	☐
_____	9. is always in the office early	☐	☐
_____	10. is a good leader	☐	☐
_____	11. makes decisions quickly	☐	☐
_____	12. has stamina for continuous hard work	☐	☐

Comments:

No: _____

_____
_____
_____
_____
_____
_____
_____
_____
_____

What makes a good time manager : commentary

As far as the ranking part of this exercise is concerned you will need to judge your choices by reference to the comments below. However, if you included point 5, that is good. Even though the rest of the comments are 'Nos', we could look at them from another direction. A couple of examples will suffice: No. 9: getting in early may just suit a person's metabolism – some of us are a.m., some p.m. people; No. 10: leadership is, as we have seen, a vital part of managerial effectiveness. A good leader will ensure that neither they nor their people will waste time. So think about these time management characteristics again, to see how you can manage your time better.

1. No. Is he or she busy doing the right things?
2. No. Most managers do. Some are good and some are bad at managing their time well.
3. No. But this could be a good sign if the supervisor is getting the job done.
4. No. But probably good at delegation!

5. Yes.
6. No. He (or she, of course) may be wasting his own time if he does not know what he should be doing.
7. No. But nice to have around.
8. No. Building barriers is a useful technique, but is he or she getting results?
9. No. May be avoiding washing up the breakfast dishes.
10. No. Nevertheless, leadership is important to a manager.
11. No. You save time in decision making by making the RIGHT decisions first time.
12. No. Stamina is invaluable – particularly if NOT managing time well.

9

Managing Change

'In turbulent times, managers cannot assume that tomorrow will be an extension of today. On the contrary, they must manage change, (both) as an opportunity and a threat.'
Peter Drucker

Managing change

Most people, consciously or unconsciously, resist change. This is often due to general feelings of insecurity, or a fear of the unknown. Changes have to be made in any organisation; internal and external conditions are always altering. Failure to change can be a recipe for disaster.

When a change has to be made, the supervisor responsible must ensure that it is both made and implemented. Plan to minimise resistance; remember, you also will not be immune to resisting change. We are all human; unfortunately our resistance tends to be much greater when change is suggested by someone else.

Essential considerations in managing change

- When discussing change, welcome the contributions of the dissenters. They make everyone else think harder; this may result in a better plan.

- There is a psychological barrier to be overcome when details of the change are being communicated to those affected (i.e. they may not understand because they do not want to understand).

- Change, whether or not necessary, is hard work; but people learn to live with change and accept it.

- Do not rush the introduction of change. 'Slow, steady and thorough' is the best way.

- If you are new in the job, be particularly careful. Until you are fully accepted, resistance to any changes you introduce will be especially strong.

- If a situation appears ripe for instant change, stop and think! The organisation has survived so far, and probably will survive for a little longer, even if you do not do anything straight away. There may be good reasons for the way things are done which will not be understood until you are fully in the picture.

- A change introduced in one part of an organisation can have more far-reaching effects and implications than the initiator realises.

- A change that appears to be minor to one person can affect a major part of some other person's role – it will thus be much more serious for them.

Management style and change

The management style that we use in the implementation of change will determine how successful we will be. There are five main styles and many sub styles.

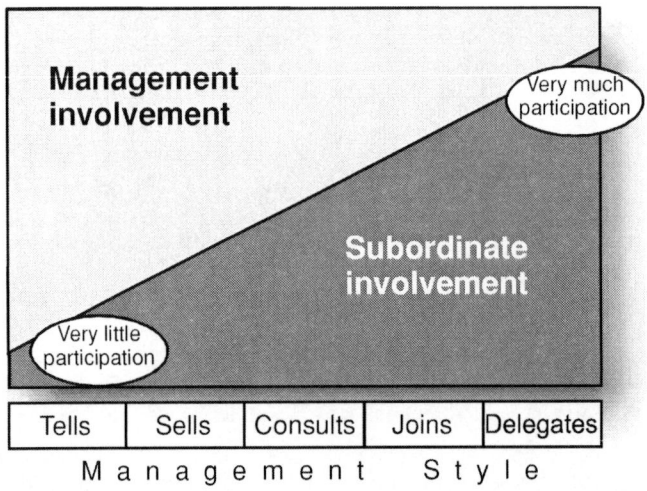

Figure 9 – Management Styles and Change

These styles are graduated from authoritative to participative. No one style is exclusive. The well-trained supervisor will use their skill and instinct to pitch the style at the best level for the circumstances.

1. **Tells**   You make the decision by yourself; then announce it to subordinates.

2. **Sells**   You make the decision; then explain it to subordinates and sell the benefits to them.

3. **Consults**   You ask for subordinates opinions; weigh up all the evidence and then make the decision yourself.

4. **Joins**   You and your subordinates discuss the matter; the decision is made according to the majority opinion.

5. **Delegates** You give one or more of your subordinates the authority to make certain decisions; do not become involved yourself.

Style 1 is 'no involvement'; style 5 is 'maximum involvement'; styles 2, 3 and 4 bridge the gap between the two extremes.

Whatever management style we follow, the change process throws up many unexpected barriers. We must always remember what makes people behave the way they do – their motivation – and behave towards them so as to persuade them to accept and implement the changes. There are pros and cons as to which style is going to be the most effective. Much depends on the circumstances. For example, in an emergency, a consultative style is not recommended. Also the personal inclination of the supervisor will often be the deciding factor in how they operate.

Authoritative and Participative management styles – advantages and disadvantages

No involvement (authoritative)

Advantages:	Disadvantages:
• Quick	• Tendency for you to seem remote from the team; special care needed to compensate for this
• People can simply be told	• No one, apart from you, gets any experience of decision making; no provision for succession or deputising.
• No arguments	• Easy to overlook something vital
• You may have specialised knowledge which subordinates do not have.	• Decisions made this way if wrong, may make subordinates disaffected and critical.

Maximum involvement (participative)

Advantages:	Disadvantages:
• Better decisions are made if more people have a chance to make suggestions, think of objections and contribute to discussions.	• Can be slow and cumbersome.
	• Effective control of the process is harder if more people are involved.
• People feel more committed to a course of action if they have had a say in deciding upon it	• Lack of objectivity about things which affects pride, ambitions or prospects; tendency to force through decisions not in line with the objectives of the organisation as a whole.
• Delegation is one of the best ways of developing people.	• An eloquent or well-liked person may sway opinion too much – a less influential individual may get no notice even if his message makes sense.

Managing change is the really tough part of the supervisor's job. Excellent communication and motivational skills are needed. One has to have a feeling of how people are being affected. Even though you may not like it yourself you nevertheless are expected to lead and persuade people to accept the uncomfortable process, which they may not see as being of benefit to them. Coming through a difficult change process with flying colours is a sure sign of a successful supervisor.

Managing Change

To get you thinking:

Checklist for the management of change

Here is a useful checklist when involved in the tricky business of introducing change. Even small changes can be difficult, so this checklist emphasises the need to get people on your side and working with you. This indicates that a consultative management style will work best; if people understand why any change is needed and can see the benefits (not necessarily just for themselves) then they will accept it more willingly. If they are simply told about it, they will resist and understandably there will be trouble. So this checklist should help in covering most points in the sequence of events that need to happen in introducing and managing change.

- Establish the objective of the proposed change; ensure that there is a good reason for it. ☐
- Collect all the relevant facts and figures. Ask all those involved for ideas, opinions, suggestions and objections. ☐
- Emphasise benefits of the change. ☐
- Foresee the problems of the change. ☐
- Plan implementation and timing of the change. ☐
- Communicate the plan to everybody concerned. Emphasise the benefits, justify the disadvantages, explain how the problems will be overcome. ☐
- Ensure that everyone knows their new role and is well trained to handle it. ☐
- Thank everyone for their assistance; explain why certain ideas and suggestions were not adopted. ☐
- Implement the change. ☐
- Check after a settling down period. Ensure that things are still going as they should. ☐
- Things will not stay changed just because you have ordered it. Constant control and follow-up is essential. ☐

10

Delegation

'If I'm being paid a dollar to do some work, I'm happy to give him five cents to do it for me.'
Mark Twain

Introduction

Delegation is giving subordinates freedom and authority to carry out some work processes on their own initiative, with confidence that they can do the job successfully.

Delegation extends the supervisor's ability to manage the job and is both an opportunity and a responsibility. Great care should be taken in how, and to whom, one delegates. The right choice of jobs for delegation is essential, as is the right choice of person and their training.

The supervisor needs to understand all aspects of the job and to consider what is possible to delegate and what is not; there are some job elements and circumstances in which it would be unfair and irresponsible to delegate. Remember too, that whatever supervisors delegate, the ultimate responsibility for the job remains theirs; it is vital therefore that delegation be done excellently.

The Story of Moses

The following story is about the first recorded incident of delegation (and management consulting).

Delegation

The Bible tells the story of Moses leading the people of Israel on their flight from Egypt. Moses, without help from any other mortal, single-handedly led the flight, parted the Red Sea, and arranged to feed the Chosen People in the wilderness. His organisation chart looked something like this:

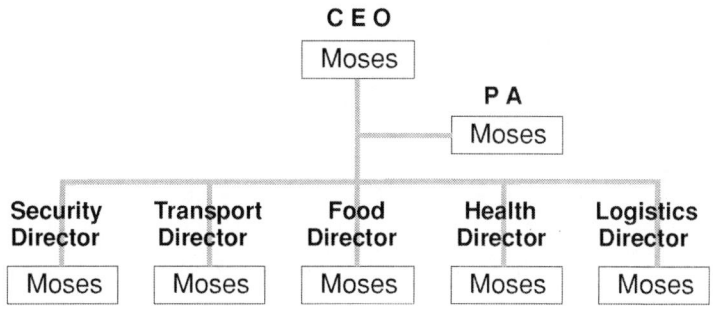

Figure 10 – Moses' delegation problem

As would be expected, Moses was very tired from handling all the problems facing him. Jethro, Moses' father-in-law, approached Moses to chide him about doing everything himself. (In-laws often offer unsolicited advice!) Jethro told Moses that what he was doing was not effective – he would wear himself out, and he was setting a bad example for the people too. He suggested Moses choose able men and place them over the people as rulers of thousands, of hundreds, of fifties, and of tens. These rulers could solve the small problems and bring only the important problems to Moses. In suggesting that Moses delegate, Jethro may have been the first management consultant in history.

Reasons why supervisors do not delegate:

Moses probably suffered from most of these problems (but with a boss like his, who can blame him!).

- **Unable or unwilling to let go:**
  - insecurity
  - lack of experience in delegating and balancing of workloads
  - perfectionism
  - fear of losing control.
- **Don't want to:**
  - enjoy doing the job themselves
  - lack of confidence in subordinates
  - like to give the impression that they are overworked and underpaid (the martyr syndrome!)
- **Fear:**
  - subordinates may make mistakes (and the supervisor will look foolish!).
  - the supervisor may appear redundant.
- Takes too much time (the supervisor can do it quicker themselves).
- No one to delegate to; no trained staff (train them!)
- Cannot trust anyone! (Learn to have confidence in your staff, get to know them.)

All these anxieties are undoubtedly justified. Insecurity is a common factor in any supervisor's working life; and we all prefer to do the things we know and like. However, to make time to do the real job, the supervisor must learn how to delegate effectively.

The delegation process

There are five distinct stages in the delegation process which lead to the supervisor being able to devolve responsibility and authority to the subordinate. Figure 11 shows the steady decrease of the supervisor's part of the job and the corresponding expansion of the subordinate's job until full ownership is achieved.

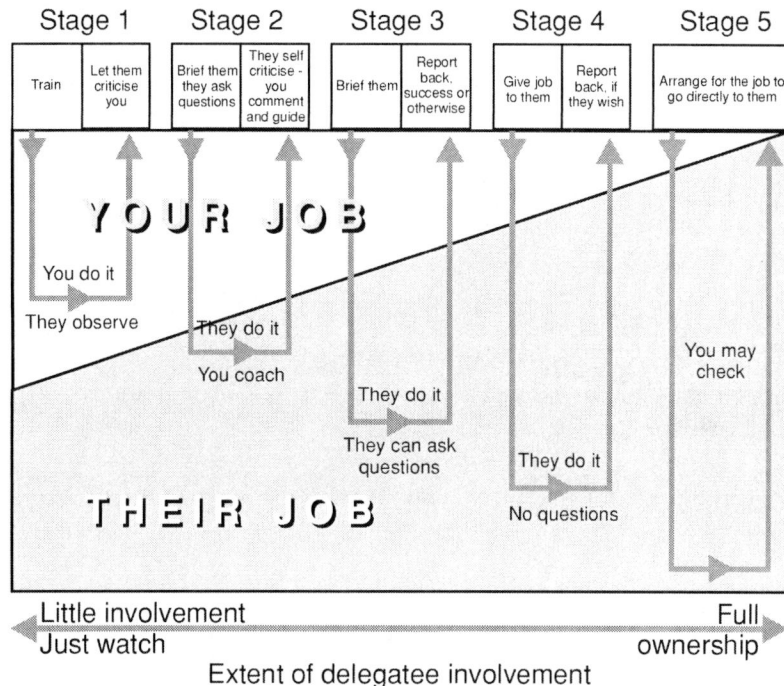

Figure 11 – The delegation process

Effective delegation

Good delegation is the best way to increase our own efficiency. We all know what delegation means, but not all of us practice it as well as we could. Delegation is most efficient when performance of a task is entrusted to a person who can do the work and the expected results are mutually understood.

To delegate effectively we should carry out the following good practices.

- **Choose the work to be delegated and choose the right person**. The person selected should be able to do the job, with guidance and training from us.

- **Define the job and ensure a clear understanding of what is expected.** Outline the job, preferably in writing, discuss the objectives, agree the standards expected. Don't merely ask if they understand, because all the pressure will be on them to say that they do understand. Ask them to explain their concept of what the job requires. Let them know that the channels of communication are open; that we will be available when needed, and that we have confidence in their ability to do the job.

- **Prepare and motivate staff.** Build people's confidence in themselves. Express your confidence in their ability. Emphasise the importance of the delegated job. Say 'This is important, which is why I'm entrusting you with it. I know you can handle it.'

- **Supervise the work properly.** Don't supervise too closely while they do the job. Encourage their independence and upward communication (but not upward delegation!) by showing interest in their ideas. They will keep us informed. If upward or reverse delegation is allowed to happen, a great deal of time will be wasted and inefficiencies occur. If you waste time solving problems for subordinates (which they ought to be able to deal with themselves) you have only yourself to blame – you have delegated poorly. Adopt the principle of: 'Don't bring me problems, bring me solutions!' Similarly, supervisors need to know their own problem-solving and responsibility level without delegating upwards needlessly.

- **Accept only completed work**, a finished job, requiring only your approval. We can't properly train staff if we accept incomplete work – it creates inefficiency for us because we have to finish the task ourselves.

Delegation advantages

- Delegation adds to the competence of our staff. One of a

supervisor's responsibilities is to train staff. They will advance more rapidly if we train them to assume greater responsibility.

- Delegation 'creates' time. Many problems find their way to us because of our position, when others contact us for advice and information. Although these various tasks end up on our desks we do not have to handle them personally. Selective delegation will give us time to work on those matters which cannot be delegated.

- Delegation gets the job done, if the work can just as well be performed by another person. Our responsibility is quality control through supervision.

- Proper delegation has a motivational effect on people. Delegating new and challenging work to less experienced people enriches their jobs and enhances the importance they attach to their positions.

- Delegating effectively requires many different skills: planning, assessing a person's potential, leading, and communicating to ensure mutual understanding of the work delegated. These are all skills which we need as supervisors.

What/what not to delegate

What to delegate:

- routine tasks (and the responsibility and decision making associated with the task)
- complete jobs (gives a sense of achievement)
- jobs that others could do better (and possibly more cheaply.)

Do not delegate:

- ultimate responsibility for the task (that is always yours)

- tasks without guidance (tell them what you want done, and how it is to be done)
- unpleasant tasks (those are really your responsibility – you cannot offload them).

How to get results through sensible delegation

When we delegate, we need to do so sensibly and not in desperation. The logical process that we go through to select what to delegate and who to delegate to needs to be reinforced by careful support. Disaster will be ensured if you 'instruct and abandon'. This can be avoided by following these steps:

- Define the task/project clearly:
    - Objectives/optimum results.
    - Importance.
    - Scope of responsibility/authority

- Think through your decision:
    - Are they trained?
    - Do they have the time?

- Think through possible training needs:
    - Direct the selected staff towards self-instruction.
    - Delegate training when possible.

- Continue to supply resources and support.
    - Never let them feel that they have been abandoned.

- Allow for maximum flexibility.
    - Discuss changes of plan to get optimum results.

- Establish a routine for your absence
    - Ask yourself:
        - What must be done while I am away?

- Who will do it?
- What authority will they have?
- What training/information do they need?

● How to delegate when you have no one to delegate to:
  ❖ Determine the Priority
    - Arrange to 'borrow' staff from a colleague
  ❖ Ask for help
    - Make a deal
    - Agree work on priorities now, in return for later deadlines on other items.

● Follow up
  ❖ Hand hold (but not too much).

Any successful supervisor will owe that success mainly to their staff. A single person cannot do everything; if they try to they will almost certainly fail – or else drop dead! Practical, well thought out, even-handed delegation, as we have shown, extends the supervisor's capabilities, but there is one more criterion that must be present: trust.

In a busy working environment, everyone needs to rely on everyone else, the supervisor most of all. If this reliance is rewarded with good, accurate, timely work, then the reliance develops into trust. Trust is a great motivator, as we shall see, but more immediately, having it enables the supervisor to delegate and be confident that, in doing so, what needs to be done, will be done satisfactorily. Delegation is not simple, and there is a complex relationship between the delegator and delegatee which the supervisor needs to work at and understand.

To get you thinking:

Checklist for delegation

Think about the points in this checklist. They are shorthand for topics discussed in this chapter. But look into each item and consider what the implicit expansion involves. For example: 'Select people ...' means that you need to know what your people can do and want to do. So you need to understand them as individuals, not just as members of your team. 'Demand finished work': it is very difficult to restrain oneself from adding the finishing touches, but you need to do so. You need to accept that the quality is sufficient (even though it is not your quality). Think of all these points in this analytical way; you will gain a greater understanding of delegation.

- List jobs that can be delegated. ☐
- Select people who are capable, willing and interested. ☐
- Explain reasons for delegating. ☐
- Explain the results that you expect. ☐
- Let go authority – but maintain responsibility overall. ☐
- Let staff establish their own priorities – and you fix deadlines. ☐
- Follow up on the task – don't abandon the delegatees, but don't stand over them either. ☐
- Be available for help when needed. Invest time in explaining and coaching. This will pay off – but don't then do the job for them (this is like buying a dog and then barking yourself). ☐
- Demand finished work. ☐
- Don't accept problems but do encourage suggestions for solutions. ☐
- Always give credit and praise for good work. ☐
- Remember intelligent people learn from their mistakes. ☐

11

Communication Skills

'Hear what you say through your listener's ears. See what you write through your reader's eyes.'

Sam Whitbread

The communication process

First, a definition:

'Transmission of ideas, feelings, information, instructions from the mind of one person (the sender) to the mind of another (the receiver), without any loss or distortion.'

The definition leads to understanding the process of:
- Thought ...
  - Coded and Sent ...
    - Received ...
      - Understood ...
        - Accepted

and provides the outline for thinking about the difficulties of effective communication and how we can overcome them. Effective communication is hard work. It is also the key to success in business, and in life. Communication is a two way process, giving and receiving; if it is simply one way, it will fail. Failure of communication means problems, which will need to be solved, and which will waste time. The successful supervisor communicates well, avoids problems and doesn't waste time.

Communication barriers

Most activities at work (or elsewhere) rely on effective communication – whether written or spoken. Often the communication process goes wrong. We do not achieve what we want because we do not overcome the barriers in the process.

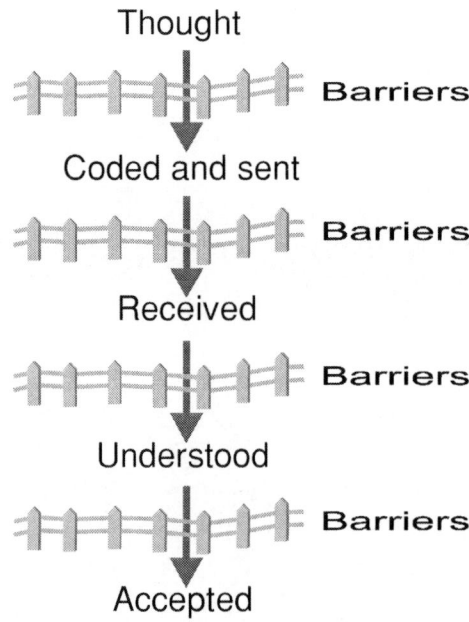

Figure 12 – Barriers to communication

Types of barrier

There are three broad categories of barriers:

Physical ('Things')
Psychological ('Feelings')
Semantic ('Words')

It may be helpful to think of these as filters, hopefully with the message getting clearer as the communication stream flows back and forth.

Physical barriers

The main ones are distance, lack of time, noise (that is, noise from outside, traffic, music and so on, or 'noise' from within: in our own heads, thoughts, daydreams, etc.), or breakdown of communications equipment. Or there may be no time for the senders to prepare their messages. So they do not organise their thoughts properly, or use words precisely.

Psychological barriers

These come from personal differences in ideas between the people communicating. Emotions, social values and differences in position in the organisation, all contribute to psychological barriers. It may be feelings about the person we are communicating with; sometimes it is our feelings towards the subject itself:

- Senders may lack a complete understanding of their own ideas; they are unlikely to be able to put them into words that can be easily and accurately understood by the receivers. They may not organise instructions in their own minds or may leave out vital pieces of information.

- Senders may be emotionally involved with the subject or the receivers. If they are excited, afraid or angry, this will affect their ability to compose the message.

- Inattention on the part of the receivers can arise because they are distracted by other thoughts about personal issues.

- A receiver may have an emotional involvement with the subject or with the person sending the message. There may be hostility towards the person sending the message.

- Other emotional states of the receivers can affect the accuracy with which they hear the message being transmitted; they may be angry or irritated, possibly because they have been interrupted in the middle of some important task.

- Whether or not the receivers understand the subject, they may lack interest in it; this will affect the level of concentration they give to the communication.

- Even though the receivers have understood the message, they may not be prepared to accept it. This may be because of personal emotional conflicts, such as having to carry out a task which they find stressful. For example, having to telephone someone known to be abrupt, unhelpful or rude.

Semantic barriers

Words rarely have a single meaning. Many words have relative meanings and are open to interpretation by the listener. Thus 'shortly' to a customer may mean 'in the next 2 or 3 days'; whereas what the organisation means is 'in the next 2 or 3 weeks'.

Sometimes senders cannot find the word needed to convey an idea. They may have a limited vocabulary. Or the receiver may have a limited vocabulary and not be able to understand the message. Limitation of vocabulary is not restricted to technical words or jargon; it also includes the use of ordinary words, regarded as common by the sender but unknown to the receiver.

There may be difficulties if the language being used is not the sender's or the receiver's mother tongue. They may not understand the words, or the words may have a different emphasis in their language.

Avoiding the barriers

To make our communications as a sender more effective, be aware of these differences. Consider ways to improve the receiver's understanding. Be aware that physical, psychological and semantic barriers exist. Plan how to overcome them in the way we communicate. Always remember that if communication doesn't succeed – it is your fault!

Overcoming communication barriers

Your position as supervisor has placed you at some level of authority over your subordinates. This in itself raises communication barriers. The anxiety of the subordinate may come through to cause communication difficulties. You therefore need to work hard to overcome these barriers. Remember, if they don't understand – it's your fault! Here are some helpful ideas:

Feedback
Make communication a two-way process. Involve the receiver and get greater commitment to understanding the message being received. To make the communication process two-way, the sender has to do more than invite questions. The receiver will not always respond to such an invitation. Encourage the two-way process by asking questions yourself, to check the receiver's understanding of the communication.

Know the receiver
Try to understand the receiver. It will be easier if you can put the communication in a way that matches their knowledge and interests. Think about the language they will understand; background knowledge; expectations; preferred methods of receiving communications; attitude to the subject and to you, the sender.

Plan communication
First ask why you are communicating. What is your purpose? Think of what the receiver is going to do as a result of your communication.

Second, consider the who of the communication; so – know the Receiver.

Third, consider the where and the when. Both are important in gaining acceptance for your message. Choose the right time, when the receiver has time and is willing to give your communication a hearing. Choose a place which will create the right environment.

Finally, how: this covers the method of the communication and the way it is expressed. It is important to:

- think clearly about what you want to say
- put the information in a logical order
- express your thoughts clearly, concisely and in words that the receiver will understand.

Written or spoken communication?

Remember the receiver, when you balance the relative advantages of the written and the spoken word for your communication. Some people prefer to see things in writing, to think about them before having a discussion. Others prefer to talk through ideas before getting a written summary. Let the receiver's preference guide your choice of method if you want your communication to be accepted, understood and acted upon.

Advantages of the spoken word
The spoken (and listened to) word:

- provides opportunity for questions, discussion and so on
- allows the speaker to assess the effect of his or her words on the listeners
- lets people feel consulted and involved
- allows for complicated matters to be talked through and fully explained
- may be seen as more 'human', less bureaucratic, by the receivers.

Advantages of the written word
The written (and read) word:
- is permanent
- is available for reference
- lets the writer choose words carefully in dealing with complex or sensitive matters
- provides evidence of information/instructions/advice given
- is convenient – can be circulated quickly among many people

- minimises overt conflict, personality clashes and so on
- is less expensive than meetings, needs fewer working hours.

The receiver's preference (if you can find out what it is) should guide your choice of method. Our communication is intended to be accepted, understood and acted upon; so it needs some effort!

Using questions creatively

There are various types of questions that can be deliberately used in order to get a full exchange of views between people. In many situations, especially in boss/subordinate ones, people are often hesitant or even fearful; this can happen on both sides. The closed question that simply gets a 'yes' or 'no' answer is appropriate sometimes. But it doesn't get very far if you are either trying to persuade, or get ideas or agreement from someone.

The following types of questions can be used to stimulate verbal communication:

Open questions
Open questions cannot be answered 'yes' or 'no' and invite a true expression of opinion and feelings, whether they are favourable or unfavourable to your point of view, e.g:

> 'What do you think of...?'
> 'How do you feel about...?'

There are several advantages to using open questions.

- They show your interest in the other person. We like having others interested in us and what we think.
- They make the other person more comfortable and secure. They allow them to direct the conversation for a time.
- They get them to think about your ideas.
- They draw them out and let you learn more about them, and

what's on their mind. The answers tell you where the real blocks to agreement are; you can design your approach more effectively.

Reflective questions

Reflective questions are the repetition or rephrasing, in your own words, of what the other person is trying to say or seems to feel. It is essential to listen carefully and select. To reflect feelings properly, really **listen**, don't think about your own plan or what you are going to say next. Then, select the most important idea or feeling from what has been said, and put it into your own words. Reflection does several things:

- It avoids argument; it enables you to respond without either rejecting or accepting what has been said.
- It shows that you understand. If your reflection is wrong, they have a chance to correct you. This goes a long way toward creating mutual understanding. There is also the ploy of the 'deliberate mistake'. Reflect incorrectly, they then correct you. This deepens understanding on both sides.
- The sharing of feelings creates a climate of agreement.
- If they have been illogical, they will be able to see the error better when it is expressed by you. Getting the other person to correct their own mistakes relieves you of this responsibility. It also avoids creating friction between you.
- A bad idea is very often forgotten after you have reflected it back. In hearing it from you, the errors can be recognised.
- Reflection enables people to pick up the main idea, they can then continue a logical progression in their thinking.
- Reflection encourages people to express themselves further, or clarify something they have previously said.

Directive questions

Directive questions request expansion or further explanation on one particular point. Hold directive questions off until you have had a complete expression of feelings and opinions, so that you understand the other person's point of view as much as possible. Directive questions keep two-way communication going, and also get clarification of some things in which you are directly interested.

- They give you more information about their thinking on points where you need such information.
- They tend to make them more favourable to your position. The more you get the other person to explore the area of agreement, the less important the area of disagreement will seem.
- They give the other person the opportunity to convince themselves. By getting them to concentrate on the positive factors, they will often realise that it is to their advantage to accept your ideas.

Redirect questions

These are a very useful, if impertinent, type of question. Simply ask, in reply to a negative statement 'Why not?' or 'Why can't we do this?' This pushes the other person into thinking about the problem again; it may relieve a deadlock. It could end up in more fruitful discussion, where both sides may be able to change their minds and get agreement.

Listening skills

Listening well is a real skill. Most people are poor listeners – they cannot concentrate for more than a few minutes, lack patience, or are too busy thinking about what they want to say next.

Here are a few guidelines to becoming a better listener:

- Let the other person finish speaking. Interrupting or completing their sentence for them, will only irritate them.
- Listen carefully to what is being said. Keep your mind clear – don't think about your next point, or you will miss what is said.
- A common mistake is to 'half listen', hearing what you want to hear, rather than what is actually said.

- Mentally summarise the most important points that the other person makes. It is a good idea to start your reply by restating these key points.
- Don't let your interpretation be distorted by your opinion or feelings about the other person, their appearance or the way they speak.
- Weigh up what is being said. Ask yourself 'Am I getting the complete picture? Does this support, or alter, my understanding?'
- Sometimes you have to look beyond the words themselves to get the real meaning. Points omitted, tone of voice, manner and facial expression can all provide added meaning.

Why we don't hear other people

To listen so that you really hear what others say, **don't** be one of the following.

- **Mind reader.** You'll hear little or nothing as you think 'What is this person really thinking or feeling?'
- **Rehearser.** Your mental tryouts for 'Here's what I'll say next' tune out the speaker.
- **Filterer.** This is selective listening – hearing only what you want to hear.
- **Dreamer.** Drifting off during a face-to-face conversation can lead to an embarrassing 'What did you say?' or 'Could you repeat that?'
- **Referencer.** If you refer everything you hear to your experience, you probably won't hear what is being said. If you try to reference everything you hear, you will be lost before you start.
- **Comparer.** When you get side-tracked assessing the messenger, you're sure to miss the message.
- **Subject changer.** Changing the subject too quickly soon tells others you're not interested in anything they have to say.
- **Arguer.** You hear what's said, but quickly belittle or discount it. That puts you in the same class as the subject changer.
- **Agreer.** Agreeing with everything you hear just to be nice or

to avoid conflict does not mean you're a good listener.

Improving one's listening skills really pays off. As well as actually understanding what is being said, and thus being in a position to respond appropriately and accurately, you win respect. The other person will feel good about communicating with you; 'you know what I'm saying, and why, and how I feel'. This attitude is the reward for the good listener. It makes life simpler too; fewer misunderstandings, hurt feelings or arguments. One has often heard of a 'dialogue of the deaf'; no one listening, nothing gets done, or progressed, and often conflict results. Listen well – manage well.

To get you thinking:

Keys to effective listening

Here are some guidelines to develop better listening habits:

Effective Listening Traits	The Poor Listener	The Effective Listener
1. Finds areas of interest.	Tunes out boring subjects (his perception).	Is an opportunist; asks 'what's in it for me?'
2. Judges content, not delivery	Tunes out if delivery is poor.	Judges content; doesn't worry about errors of delivery.
3. Holds fire.	Gets into arguments.	Doesn't judge until he has complete comprehension.
4. Listens for ideas.	Listens for facts.	Listens for central themes.
5. Is flexible.	Takes intensive notes; uses only one system.	Takes fewer notes. Uses different systems, depending on speaker.
6. Works at listening.	Shows no energy output. Attention is faked.	Works hard, exhibits active body state.
7. Resists distractions.	Distracted easily.	Fights or avoids distractions, tolerates bad habits, knows how to concentrate.
8. Exercises mind.	Resists difficult material; seeks light, recreational material.	Uses heavier material as exercise for the mind.
9. Keeps mind open.	Reacts to emotional words.	Interprets colours, words; does not get hung up on them.
10. Capitalises on the fact that thought is faster than speech.	Tends to daydream with slow speakers.	Challenges, anticipates, mentally summarises, weighs the evidence, listens between the lines to tone of voice

12

Non-verbal Communication

'There's no art to find the mind's construction in the face.'
William Shakespeare

People often do not mean what they say. Often their real attitude and feelings are shown by subconscious gestures and postures.

A basic understanding of non-verbal communication will help anyone become a more effective communicator. You will have a greater understanding of other people; be able to put yourself in the other person's shoes. For example: someone may sound very keen about a proposal you are making or a service you are offering. Actually they are evaluating you very carefully. They may sound friendly, but the non-verbal communications show suspicion.

Non-verbal communications include signs of reassurance, nervousness, frustration, confidence, co-operation and territorial dominance. Remember, however, these signs are only a guide – they are not infallible. We all make gestures to some extent and hand gesturing when speaking can relax you. It reinforces your message and makes you more interesting to listen to.

Some tips:

- Open your arms as if to embrace your listeners; but keep your arms between shoulders and waist where your listener can see them.
- Drop your arms to your sides when not using them.
- Avoid quick jerky gestures; they make you appear nervous. Don't hold gestures long in normal conversation; you become theatrical!

- Vary gestures. Switch hands and at times use both or no hands.

But take care not to overuse gestures.

Body Language

Body language is the only language which is spoken by everybody, but understood by only a few. Less than 10% of the impression you get of another person is created through the words they say. The way things are said is much more important. So is the voice, the speed, and the body language, which give more than half of the impression made. Body language is all the things you notice about the people in a television programme when the volume is turned down.

All the people you communicate with: business associates, the opposite sex, salespeople, politicians, family members, bosses and colleagues – speak a non-verbal language with their body. This language reveals what they actually mean more than all the words in the world.

At some point in any interaction, the brain will adopt a complex of attitudes and positions. These communicate from the brain to the various parts of the body, with orders to take a particular stance or make a specific gesture. What the body does, becomes the body language; these gestures and signals are communicated to other people – often unconsciously.

Words may lie; the body seldom does!
Movements, body posture, sitting posture, position of the arms, facial expressions, eye movements, handshakes, walk and so on – these are all body language indicators. Of great importance also are very small and ordinary gestures and signals, which are frequently only registered weakly, if not completely ignored.

It requires quite a bit of practice to learn to interpret other people's body language. When you are able to interpret body language, you can sense whether people are lying, are bored or impatient; feel attracted by you or the opposite; or are in a defensive position; or just waiting to 'wipe the floor with you'. You can tell whether they disagree or agree with you, whether they are open, nervous, evaluating, suspicious, angry, worried, insecure. You can also learn to sense the hidden social, emotional, sexual and other intentions which underlie the gestures of people you know or would like to know better.

Deciphering other people's body language is one thing, but it is just as important to master your own and be aware how much it means to the impression you make on others. In actors, teachers, waiters and salespeople, you can find clear examples of the importance of body language. The words used are often almost the same, irrespective of who is playing the part. The difference as to whether they play their roles well or poorly is to be found in their ability to master the body language. When you have learned to 'speak' body language, the door will be open to an entirely new dimension of communication. Obviously you have to remain in the context of your occupation; for the supervisor this will be the shop floor, the office and so on. People react to the situation they find themselves in; if the supervisor can, by using body language, open up the atmosphere a little then better results will surely happen.

When you interpret body language, it is important that you do not look at one single detail and then draw a lot of conclusions on that alone. Try to evaluate body signals as a whole and compare them with the overall situation. In order to make an evaluation with a fairly high degree of certainty, at least two or three separate elements should point to the same interpretation.

To get you thinking:

Try this to get a grip on body language:

Stand in front of a full-length mirror, normally dressed and recite from memory or read a piece of prose or poetry – a scene from a play perhaps. Watch yourself as you speak – difficult perhaps but not impossible. You will see the unconscious gestures you make, and (you are not doing this out of vanity) the facial expressions that you make as you try to get across a meaning in the text.

It may be best to do this alone!

It may be misconstrued if you too obviously closely watch people with whom you are not directly involved. So watch a television game show or soap with the sound off. Of course the people are actors, but you will be able to pick up repeated gestures and postures which you can interpret. Or if you go to a foreign film, just watch the people, don't read the subtitles; you will get the story line without the words.

Watch, interpret and learn. We all have the skill – if we hone it a bit sharper, we will be able to do our job better.

13

Effective Meetings

'... Yes, I come very often, but I have no time to read the programme; one merely comes to meet one's friends and show that one's alive ...'

Fanny Burney

Meetings, bloody meetings!

Meetings are an essential part of everyday business life. But many meetings are unnecessary, unproductive and often a waste of time. So think carefully before setting up a meeting and don't call a meeting to decide something you could and should decide yourself. And never get people together if a conference phone call to individuals would serve your purpose. Remember their time is your money.

So the next time you are sitting in a meeting wondering what on earth you are doing there, do a little positive mind wandering. Calculate what you earn on an hourly basis, then double it for the overhead costs of having you there. Then do the same, estimating earnings, for all the other people present. Add it all up and it comes to a worrying amount of money, doesn't it? Multiply this by all the other useless meetings that you attend in the course of a year, and it becomes plain why effective meetings are essential for good management.

An effective supervisor will know that good meetings are planned, they don't just happen. They start well before the participants assemble, and continue after they leave.

Run properly meetings can be an effective means of:

- communicating to a group
- meeting people face to face
- improving the quality of decisions
- getting to know people
- drawing from a variety of different experiences, and
- building teams.

There are some useful techniques that you can apply.

Before the meeting:

- Consider who you are going to invite. What will they have to contribute by way of information, opinion or assistance in the decision making? If they are not needed, don't invite them. If you are invited, apply the same criterion to your own attendance: if it comes out negatively, decline or send a well-briefed subordinate. This will save your time, and will give your subordinate good experience in attending meetings.

- Think out the agenda carefully. Define the purpose of the meeting and state it clearly: e.g. to analyse, inform, decide co-ordinate. Put the purpose at the top of your invitation memo. Likewise, if you receive an invitation to a meeting which does not state a purpose, query it. If you don't get a satisfactory answer, don't go; don't waste your time – remember how much it costs.

- Now organise the agenda. Prioritise the items, and give a very brief (no more than 10 – 12 words) statement why each item is included. Put a time limit on each item for discussion according to its importance. There should be no surprises, so those attending will have the opportunity to be prepared for the topic and contribute usefully. If the invitation that you receive is not clear as to topics and timing, seek clarification and ask approximately when the items in which you are involved will come up. Send the agenda out in good time; not too early since people forget, but not too late – don't provide an excuse for coming to the meeting unprepared.

- This leads to the idea of staggering the attendance; there is usually no need for everybody to be there all the time. Note beside each agenda item who will be involved. Try to group items together that concern an individual supervisor and get them dealt with, then they can go. It will not always work but, if they know the timing, people can come in when their item is due for discussion, slip out when it finished, and return if need be later on. It is amazing what can be done in your own office in 15 or 30 minutes when you are not being bored in an ineffective meeting.

- The timing of any meeting is important. It will be impossible to find a time that will suit everyone but, if adequate notice is given, participants will be able to organise themselves to attend without having to disrupt their schedules. Try not to hold 'emergency' meetings; but if an emergency does arise, hold a 'stand-up' meeting – don't sit down – brief people quickly on the problem and then send out action minutes. Always follow these up. Try to hold your meetings somewhere other than in your office; but if this is not possible, make sure you avoid interruptions. Put a *Do Not Disturb* sign on the door, disconnect the phone and make yourself unavailable: but let your secretary or colleagues know when you will be free. With such excellent pre-planning you will be able to tell exactly when this will be.

During the meeting:

- Start on time. Don't penalise those arriving on time and reward latecomers by waiting for them. A good chairman will be in control of the meeting at all times, and starting on time is a vital control point.

- Organise the minute taking and the time keeping. It is best not to take minutes yourself, since you need to concentrate on direction and not interrupt the flow. An independent reminder of the times you pre-set for discussion is also valuable and is a good discipline for yourself. This is particularly important if people are to join the meeting at various times. Good orchestration of a meeting generally means that it will be effective and that things will get done.

- Start with and stick to the agenda; don't be side-tracked. How you handle discussion of the topics will depend on the purpose of the meeting – to inform, generate creative solutions, or decide; different styles of chairmanship will be appropriate. But always remember the time limits that you set and the purpose of the meeting; remind everyone of this frequently.

- At the end of each item – and also at the end of the meeting – summarise, get agreement as to whether the purpose has been achieved, state conclusions, and action assignments if relevant.

- End on time; respect the plans of those who have assumed that it will, and have trusted you to achieve this aim.

After the meeting:

- Evaluate it for your own benefit, being as objective as you possibly can. Ask:
    - ❖ was the advance information adequate?
    - ❖ did the meeting start on time?
    - ❖ was the agenda followed, and was the purpose achieved in the time allocated?
    - ❖ were the right people in attendance?
    - ❖ was time wasted?

There could be more questions, but this self-evaluation is a useful learning tool for improving meeting effectiveness.

Effective Meetings

- Make sure the Minutes are sent out within two days of the meeting; the quicker the better. Minutes should be concise; they are not a verbatim record of the discussion: only decisions, those responsible for taking action, and deadlines are needed. The rest is just padding. Follow up on decisions and check what progress has been made – are there any reports, and what actions has been taken to implement decisions?

Finally ask: Is your meeting really necessary? Make a list of meetings, apply the criteria of achievement of purpose and implementation of decisions. If the meetings pass the acid test, they can continue. If they fail, disband the committee concerned, and don't allow new ones to reform by inertia. Get rid of what is unnecessary; you will save a lot of time and ensure much more effective meetings.

To get you thinking:

Checklist for successful meetings

- Hold them only if they are really needed or necessary

  (Ask yourself if people could be told any other way?)
- Set a purpose
  - What do you want to achieve?
  - What decisions need to be made?
  - What actions need to be taken?
- Consider the costs
  - Meetings aren't cheap (time away from job, salaries of those attending etc.)
- Prepare an agenda
  - Include only relevant items.
  - Put them in order of importance.
  - Allocate time for each.
- Collect all information
  - If it's lengthy summarise it, outlining key points.
  - Send out agendas and key points in advance.
  - Only invite those affected by topics under discussion.

Checklist for running the meeting

- Tell everyone the purpose.
- Set the scene for each item, e.g.
  - Open discussion by inviting specific contributions from those present. (Set time limits.)
- Let everyone who has something to say make a contribution (but watch windbags!)

- Watch for signs of non-participation. (Encourage, by open questions.)
- Summarise what has been said as the meeting proceeds. Record and ensure minutes are taken accurately.
- Stick to time (always start on time and don't be afraid to finish early).
- Agree actions to follow.
- Don't be afraid to critique the meeting:-
  - Was it worth it?
  - What could you have done differently?
- After the meeting
  - Circulate minutes to those attending and interested parties.
  - Monitor and review progress of any actions decided.

14

Presentation Skills

'Speak the speech, I pray you, trippingly on the tongue ...'
William Shakespeare

Introduction

There are only three rules for effective presentation: **preparation, practice, projection**.

Talking to a group of any size, especially if they are strangers, is a major source of anxiety for anyone, including supervisors. Which means that learning to control your nerves and 'take the floor' comfortably will give you a tremendous advantage. You need to learn techniques that well-known speakers use to relax – connect naturally – and project the relaxed presence of a confident expert.

Even the best ideas are not worth much if you cannot get people to believe in them, and in you. You need to get listeners on your side (we've talked about listening skills already) and develop credibility in your ideas, create alliances, and generate the kind of support and co-operation that get your ideas off the ground and into action.

Presenting a project on behalf of your team is a big responsibility. Others are counting on you to discuss the group's activities, project enthusiasm and report your progress accurately. If you accept this challenge with confidence, you will earn your group's admiration.

What the listener sees and hears

There are many kinds of presentations, from standing with a pointer and a flipchart in front of a group, or the presenter's group may be seated around a table in a meeting. In either case, when one person is trying to persuade one or more people, using information, there is a presentation situation.

The average person can manage a reasonable conversation with an individual, but when that person becomes part of an audience, the average person may lose his or her self-confidence. This is normally due to nervous tension, caused by:

- fear of looking foolish
- fear of failure
- fear of forgetting.

Deal with these fears through good preparation and be observant; keep sharpening your presentation skills by watching other presenters.

'To fail to prepare, is to prepare to fail.'

A presenter's nervousness will tend to worry the average listener; manner and mannerisms will be visual distractions. Remember the listeners will:

- look first ... then
- notice ... and after that
- listen.

The first step is to get on to the platform, or stand up in front of the group. Remember to relax, smile, look purposeful, shake hands mentally with the audience. Wait five seconds (count!) looking confident, then start. If your group are seated around a table – take your time. Push back your chair, rise as if you are welcoming a friend into your office, survey the group for a moment – then start.

But you can still commit faults with hands and mannerisms that will distract, and possibly irritate, the audience. The best positions for your hands are by the sides, relaxed (very difficult); clasped in front, or behind; jacket pocket (informal occasions). Feet should be placed one in front of the other at about a 45° angle with your weight equally distributed. This avoids looking like a stork and you will not suffer from pins and needles.

Also don't distract your audience by being a 'leaner and swayer', 'fidget', 'nose blower' or 'cougher', 'clock watcher', 'looker downer and arounder', 'furniture remover'. It is all too easy to build barriers to communicating with your listeners that will distract them, and may stop them listening, or even trying to listen, to your presentation.

The solution is relaxation, practice and being continually aware of the traps. We all have our individual mannerisms that we must control when we are in public. You must get the full attention of the audience; even the most experienced speakers are nervous to some degree, but if your attitude is right, your nervousness won't show and the audience will want to listen.

Good delivery

Words are the raw material of speaking; your voice is the instrument for shaping the material. If we are to do well in verbal communication, we must try to improve both factors. This does not mean standardising speech. Clear accents and dialects add colour and can be an advantage to the speaker, provided that the audience can understand the spoken word.

Practice is essential. There are five main techniques for good voice and effective use of words.

- **Good stance** will help self-confidence, help make gestures full and relevant, and help to avoid striking a 'false attitude'.
- **Correct breathing** means controlled breathing; a relaxed body with deep breathing will help to ensure maximum motive power behind the words.
- **Effective use of consonants.** Sounds like P, B, T, D, Ch, K,

L, M, N, Ng etc. This will give clarity to the presentation and a muscular outline.
- **Effective use of vowels.** Sounds like A, E, I, O, U. This gives beauty to a speech and aids audibility. To use the sounds effectively your tongue, jaw and lips must be flexible.
- **Good delivery.** The best expression of our thoughts which colour our words.
  - This is helped by the correct pitch. Try to sound natural with no strain or artificiality.
  - Use emphasis to help delivery.
  - Use inflection – try not to 'drop' at the end of every sentence.
  - Tone quality – sound sincere and enthusiastic.
  - Vary your pace and use pauses for the maximum effect (don't be frightened by silence).

The effective presenter uses words to their greatest advantage. Good phrasing helps fluency; correct pronunciation and accentuation helps the effectiveness of words. Think out the best order for words. Avoid clichés, slang, pompous phrases and technical language for non-technical people.

To increase the effective use of your voice and words:

- practice deep controlled breathing
- practice reading aloud for ten minutes every day
- practice the use and formation of words
- practice 'speaking forward' – projection.

When using a microphone, the characteristic of your voice may be changed by the acoustics of the room, or distortion caused by the microphone itself. Try to practice with the microphone before giving the presentation. Test out the room to make sure that the microphone is positioned correctly; listen to the person using the microphone before you – notice the changes in voice. Present the material more slowly and with precision in the forming of each individual word. Take your time and give the impression of confidence and control.

Presentation planning

No presentation can be better than the preparation which precedes it. But most presenters do too much work on their presentations. They gather too much information that isn't relevant to their objective. However, the presentation will be affected by the audience. Study their background, prior knowledge and attitude. Advance written material can change the audience's prior knowledge and attitude.

The 'Basic Relevance' Test

- What conclusions must I leave in my audience's mind in order to achieve my objective? (Make a clear statement of what the presentation is to achieve.)

- What information do I have to give to prove these conclusions? (This should be audience orientated and realistic.)

Presentation planning has five stages

- **Initial preparation**
  - When and where will it take place?
  - Who will be present?
  - Why me?

- **Objective?**

It is very important to have the objective of the presentation clearly defined in your own mind. Is it:
  - to inform? Use appropriate language, anecdotes and illustrations to give life and colour.
  - to persuade? Appeal to the heart and head. Quote evidence, statistics, authoritative opinions. Any data must be accurate.
  - to entertain? Be 'light', talk in terms of audience interest; relate the speech to the occasion.
  - to inspire? Quote facts, ask for action. Keep it brief and make sure that you appear to feel strongly about the matter.

- **Gathering material.** There are three main sources:
  - your own knowledge
  - other people
  - researching data from reference systems and libraries.

- **Organising material.** Observe the rules of:
  - relevance
  - priority
  - coherence
  - use of time.

- Then **write out** the presentation in note form.

Notes

Every speaker need some method of remembering what to say, how to say it and when to say it. Be professional in your approach to aids; don't pretend that you don't need them or try to hide them.

Some speakers simply read their scripts out. This ties the presenter to the 'sheets' and often to the spot. It is not a confidence builder with the audience and does not encourage questions (fear of losing your place!). Those presenters who learn their script off by heart lack flexibility, are not prepared for interruptions and can also be vocally monotonous and very boring.

Presenters who rely on scribbled notes on the back of an envelope do not inspire confidence either. But the presenter who pretends 'impromptu' is normally very well prepared. Few speakers are gifted and experienced enough to speak in public with minimum preparation and aids.

We need a method that enables us to be flexible (allowing us to answer questions), to ensure that we do not forget anything, to enable us to maintain eye contact, and to enable us to move around when necessary.

An answer is the '**Key Sentences**' technique. Each key sentence should convey a complete thought or idea, and be reinforced with the supporting points that need to be covered. These can be written on **Confidence Cards**. Of all methods, the small filing cards work best. They give us something to do with our hands, other than fidget, and are brief enough to act as clear prompts. Make sure the cards are numbered in case they are dropped and become muddled!

Making a presentation can be a daunting experience for a novice supervisor, or even a well-seasoned one. But it is one of the roles of the job, and if done well can even become enjoyable! We are none of us trained actors – that is not why we were hired. Also for many of us 'putting ourselves forward' is something that was trained out of us in childhood. Nevertheless we can learn how to do it, and do it reasonably well.

There isn't really anything to be afraid of. They – your audience – are only people like you after all. Nevertheless, it is well researched that public speaking is highly stressful, so no one is going to blame you if you are anxious. Practice makes, if not perfect, at least a lot better. And the more you can practice, the easier it becomes; take whatever opportunity comes along to speak in public – as we said, you might get to enjoy it.

To get you thinking:

How to sharpen your presentation skills

Practice is the key word and good presentation is a skill that can be learned.

Try reading some famous speeches, Churchill's for instance. Then try reading them aloud, perhaps standing in front of a mirror.

Record yourself speaking and analyse the tapes with a friend. Watch (or rather listen) for indistinct speech, poor or unclear pronunciation and fading cadences. If you do not think it is too voyeuristic, have yourself videoed either practicing or actually giving a presentation. Analyse the tape noting speech faults and also body language and gestures. It may be painful, but all this gives the best sort of feedback to help make your presentations better.

An effective public speaker keeps the audience amused; that does not mean that you have to be a stand-up comic. It does mean that you have to have something worthwhile listening to and an attractive way of saying it. So practice delivery, and if your tapes or video show a dull or monotonous delivery, train yourself out of it by listening to some really good presenters (the BBC announcers for example). Follow their cadences as good examples, and people will listen to what you have to say with interest, rather than resignation. And yes, it is OK to tell a joke or two, but make them relevant to your subject, otherwise you will probably confuse the audience.

15

Motivation and Expectations

'... it is not profit as such, that makes the business person tick, it is the strong desire for achievement ...'

David C. McClelland

Motivation in the work situation

What is motivation?
Motivation is the feeling of commitment to doing something well, and being prepared to put energy and effort into it. It varies in nature and intensity from individual to individual, and on the particular mixture of influences at any given moment. These relate to the person's needs. It is, as McClelland puts it, the desire for achievement and the need to feel good about oneself and what one is doing.

Motivation is vital in any job if an individual is to give his or her best to it. Assuming that employees are given ample opportunity for good performance (correct tools, work method and so on) and have the necessary skills, then effectiveness depends on their motivation. Getting people to the place of work ensures attendance. What matters is getting them to work willingly, with effort and effectiveness while they are there.

Signs of motivation
Attitudes and behaviour at work reflect motivation – or lack of it. Indications of motivation will be seen for example in:

- high performance/results achieved
- energy, enthusiasm and determination
- co-operation in overcoming problems
- willingness to accept responsibility/accommodate change.

Lack of motivation will be indicated by:

- poor timekeeping/high absenteeism
- apathy and indifference
- exaggeration of disputes/grievances
- uncooperativeness/resistance to change.

It is the supervisor's job to motivate the team as far as possible, being best placed to create the environment in which people will give their best to their work. Some factors are outside their control, e.g. pay, status, terms and conditions of employment. But, responsibility, challenging work and opportunities for growth and development are in the supervisor's hands. Research and practical experience have shown these to be the most important motivating factors.

Practical steps in motivation

The supervisor must know how to get people to work willingly and well, so as to increase the individual's satisfaction in his job, and the organisation's efficiency. To do this, the supervisor must practice the following vital concepts.

Make subordinates feel valued
- Regularly monitor the subordinates work.
- Share an interest in whatever they hold important.
- Create an atmosphere of approval and co-operation.
- Ensure understanding of the importance of their contribution to the team's objectives, and the function of the organisation.

Provide scope for development
- Set targets for all subordinates.
- Provide on and off the job training.
- Arrange any necessary internal and external contacts.
- Use subordinates to train others in the specialist skills they may have.
- Group tasks to use subordinates skills to the fullest.

Recognise achievements
- Praise and communicate individual successes.
- Report regularly on the team's progress.
- Hold regular meetings to monitor and counsel on an individual's progress towards targets.
- Explain the company results and achievements.

Provide challenge
- Set and communicate the team's objectives.
- Provide scope for individuals to take greater responsibility.
- Fully train at least one deputy.
- Encourage ideas and, where practical, allow subordinates the responsibility for implementing them.

Recognition – the vital element
Of all the ways that a supervisor can motivate staff, recognition is the most important. People need to feel that they are appreciated for what they are and what they do. The idea of recognition is implicit in all these practical steps and it is a vital management tool which contributes to effective and profitable performance.

> *'Well-managed people are well-motivated people.*
> *Well-motivated people are happy people.*
> *Happy people work well and are productive.*
> *Productive people make profits.'*
>
> Lord Sieff

Motivation theories

Three major theories of motivation follow. In some ways they each state the same things. It is certainly worthwhile understanding these basic statements about motivation. Observe, and you will see how true they are; use them well and greatly improve your own skills in motivation.

These are, of course, not the only theories, but perhaps not surprisingly, most are mainly commentaries upon those presented here. Fundamentally motivation is fairly simple: find out what makes people happy (silly word?) and if all's well, they will behave in a rational and productive way. If people are not happy then the rationality starts to break down; they begin to behave in an 'equalising' way so as to balance their discontent with their circumstances. This is a situation that the supervisor should try to avoid; watch for the signs and, if you know your Maslow, McGregor and Herzberg, you will have a good idea of what is going on – and (perhaps) be able to stop a real problem developing.

Abraham Maslow: The needs hierarchy

Maslow compiled what he called the Hierarchy of Needs. This lists the basic human needs and indicates the sequence in which they are likely to assume importance:

- **Physical** needs (food, shelter, sex).
- **Security** needs (physical or social security).
- **Social** needs (the need to be accepted, to belong).
- **Ego satisfying** needs (the need for recognition and esteem).
- **Self-fulfilment** needs (the need to develop as a person).

The concept indicates that, as the more basic needs are satisfied, the more sophisticated needs become more important as motivators. However, even someone who has developed to the more sophisticated level of need, should they suddenly lose the means of satisfying not only these, but also the basic ones, they will immediately become concerned with fulfilling physical and security needs again.

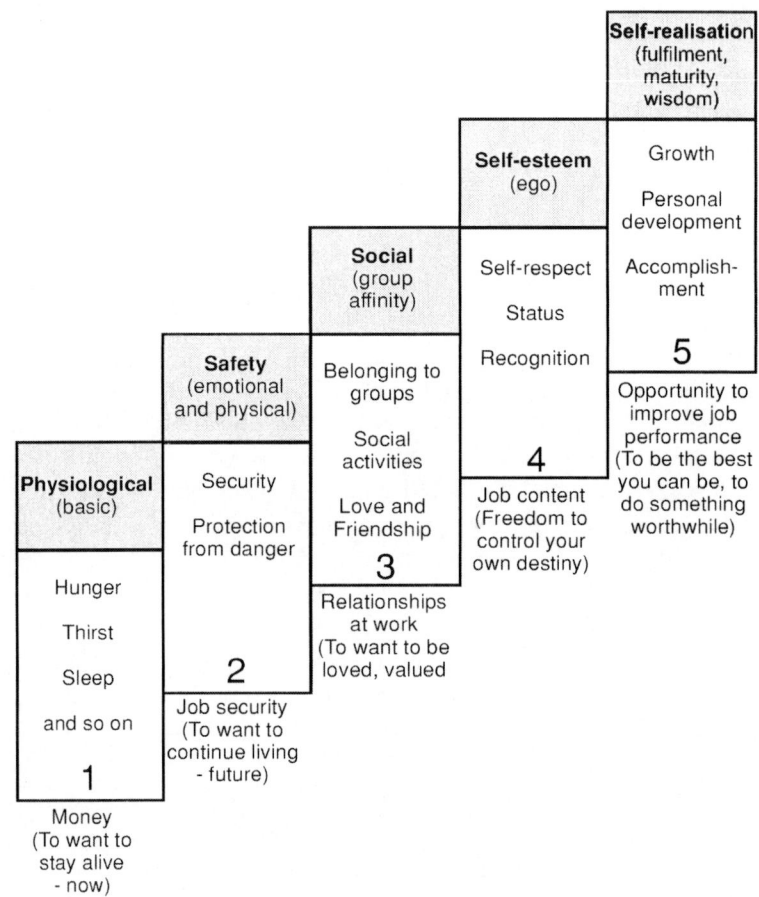

Figure 13 – Maslow's hierarchy of needs

Individual needs

- They are based on needs not wants.

- They operate on an ascending scale. As one need becomes fulfilled, the next ascendant need is uncovered.

- Needs 'revert back', i.e. people operating at level 4 or 5 will revert to level 2 if a feeling of insecurity takes over. Once this need is met however individuals will return to their former needs area.

- Needs not being met are demonstrated in behaviour. Managers must create an 'environment' in which motivation can take place.

- To avoid apathy (which results when needs are unfulfilled), managers must be able to implement the right action at the right time.

People's attitude to work (the X – Y theory)

Managers make assumptions about people at work. Douglas McGregor described these as theory X and theory Y.

These are the X and Y factors:

Theory X

- People dislike work and will avoid it if they can.
- People must be forced or bribed to put out the right effort.
- People would rather be directed than accept responsibility, which they avoid.
- People are motivated mainly by money.
- People are motivated by anxiety about their security.
- People have little creativity – except when it comes to getting round management rules!

Theory Y

- Work is necessary to people's psychological growth.
- People want to be interested in their work and, under the right conditions, they can enjoy it.
- People will direct themselves towards an accepted target.

- People will seek, and accept responsibility under the right conditions.
- The discipline people impose on themselves is more effective, and can be more severe, than any imposed on them.
- Under the right conditions, people are motivated by the desire to realise their own potential.
- Creativity and ingenuity are widely distributed and grossly underused.

If we assume X, and we treat people accordingly, we find out nothing about them. Our beliefs become a self-fulfilling prophecy, i.e. people will need close supervision, firm discipline, incentive schemes and so on.

If, however, we believe that Y is correct and treat people accordingly, we find out what they are really like. The answer will be that they are all different and we can then manage them according to their strengths and weaknesses.

The key is, don't make assumptions, give opportunity for achievement, responsibility, creativity and so on.

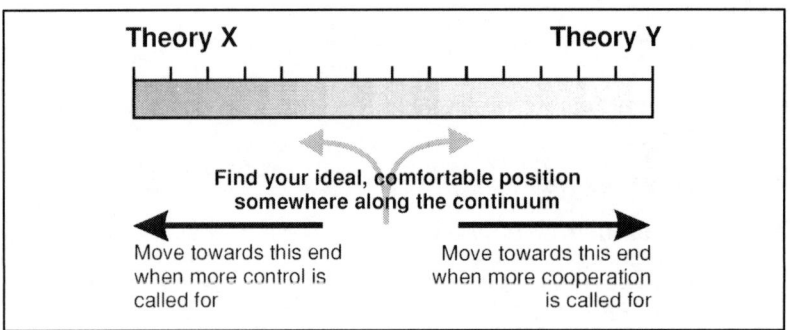

Figure 14 – Theory X and Y

If you imagine theory X at one end of a scale and theory Y at the other, in all probability your personal view will set your own attitude to your staff somewhere between the two. There will be occasions when you need to move strongly towards X (as, for instance, when dealing with a disciplinary situation); or maybe you will need to move nearer to Y (as when trying to put across a difficult change to procedures). Whatever your personal style, your staff will be happier if they recognise it and you do not wander back and forth along the scale without good reason.

Herzberg: satisfaction and dissatisfaction (motivation and hygiene factors)

Frederick Herzberg asked many people in different jobs at different levels two questions:

- What factors lead you to experience extreme dissatisfaction with your job?
- What factors lead you to experience extreme satisfaction with your job?

He identified a number of factors which lead to job satisfaction and job dissatisfaction. The collated answers show the order and frequency in which the factors appeared.

Potential satisfiers (motivators)	Potential dissatisfiers (hygiene factors)
• Achievement • Recognition • Work itself • Responsibility • Advancement • Growth	• Company policy and administration • Supervision • Interpersonal relations • Work conditions • Salary • Security
Job satisfaction (motivators)	**Job dissatisfaction (demotivators)**

Figure 15 – Motivators and hygiene factors

Dissatisfaction (hygiene factors)

The factors on the right side of the chart tend to cause dissatisfaction rather than satisfaction. Further investigation showed that the dissatisfaction was only present where the factor (e.g. salary) was not fulfilling the expectation of the employee. If the factor was changed to the employee's expectation, it merely disappeared as a source of unhappiness. It did not create satisfaction. Another important point in these factors is that they are all concerned with what is done to or for an employee, or is concerned with relationships over which they do not have full control.

Satisfaction (motivators)

Factors on the left side of the chart have little to do with money and status. They have much to do with achievement and responsibility. They are connected with the job content, i.e. the things that people do at work. These factors were identified as providing greatest satisfaction at work.

The moral for supervisors is clear; pay particular attention to the kind of tasks people are expected to do. Job satisfaction comes from our involvement in doing what we think is worthwhile and challenging.

> Note: Herzberg's findings have recently been updated by surveying people at work in 22 countries. The findings are absolutely consistent with the original research.

Ways to effectively demotivate

Unfortunately there are more ways to *demotivate* people than to motivate them. Sometimes it is our unconscious or thoughtless words or actions which put people off. It is only too easy to do some of the things listed below. So if you, as a supervisor, find yourself doing any (or all!) of these things – **DON'T!**

- Don't take them into your confidence, keep them in the dark about the real purpose of their work.

Motivation and Expectations

- Make sure you get credit while they get the blame.
- Never admit that you might be wrong.
- Don't give them sincere praise.
- Put them on work for which they are temperamentally unsuited.
- Let them get involved in a really serious mistake before you pull them up.
- Talk about 'objectives', '£/$ results', but make it quite clear that not rocking the boat and conforming to the system is really much more important.
- If they come to you for real help, give them platitudes.
- Harp on details while ignoring the real issues.
- Avoid giving advance information about changes that affect them.
- Discourage new ideas.
- Insist that they do the job your way.
- Make it clear that it never pays to step out of line.
- Demonstrate that promotion goes to those who ingratiate themselves rather than those who perform.

Every one of these actions is a **cardinal sin of management**. If you really want demotivated staff, go ahead, practice these boorish actions. If you, on the other hand, want well motivated, productive staff, avoid these actions like the plague.

Create the right climate

In order to motivate successfully, a supervisor has to be able to recognise the basic human needs and to be aware of the process of motivation. It is useless to make a spasmodic approach to motivation: it is a continuing task of management and the first rule is to establish the **right climate**. To create this:

- encourage a sense of the importance of the job
- develop a sense of involvement amongst subordinates
- give evidence of management efficiency
- display evidence of management openness
- create a sense of teamwork and team identity.

Respect subordinates as individuals and get to know what motivates each one. This must be on a continual basis; when motivation is the issue the supervisor is always on duty.

Expectations

The concept of expectations is sometimes called the Pygmalion effect. The basic idea is that other people may fulfil our expectations; if our expectations are positive they will succeed; if our expectations are negative they may fail. It does not always turn out this way, but it occurs more often than we realise.

The Pygmalion effect

Pygmalion was a sculptor in Greek mythology. He carved a statue of a beautiful woman that was subsequently brought to life. George Bernard Shaw's play 'Pygmalion' (the basis for the musical 'My Fair Lady'), has a similar theme. The essence is that one person, by his effort and will, can transform another person.

In the world of management, many supervisors play Pygmalion-like roles in developing able subordinates and in stimulating their performance. What is the secret of their success? How are they different from supervisors who fail to develop top-notch subordinates?

> *'It's all quite simple; if you're someone who's important to them, normal people tend to meet your expectations of them. Not all of them. Not all the time. But pretty generally they will. If you degrade them constantly, they'll degrade themselves. If you tell them you expect good things to come from them, and if they believe you, then pretty soon you'll start to see good things coming from them.'*
>
> George V. Higgins

Some bosses please or disappoint us when they exceed, or fail to meet, our expectations. The more effective boss recognises our expected needs for challenges, a chance to achieve, for praise, for recognition and involvement. Ineffective bosses suffer because they expect too much or too little, or because they make us feel unimportant or incompetent.

There are difficulties in fulfilling expectations; for instance:-

- If you become more positive in your approach to people, maybe you will become unrealistic in your thinking, as will the person who becomes more negative. There are risks either way, in being positive or negative. The problem is to determine which risk is greater. Or ...

- Should you ignore the mistakes of subordinates in your effort to become less negative? The question is, does an effective boss side-step reality?

The answers will always depend on circumstances and personalities. But the reality is that expectations are always there, and have a decided effect on our motivation.

Good Practice
To fulfil people's expectations the following points are essential.

- Different people have different expectations.

- People expect **us** to live up to **their** expectations.

- The supervisor needs to be aware of the different expectations of the individual and the team.

- To satisfy all, or some, of the various expectations, the supervisor will have to be sufficiently flexible to change behavioural styles, as people and circumstances demand.

- Ignoring any one group's expectations completely, or for too long a period, will almost certainly result in a backlash of some kind.

- Supervisors have the same values and expectations as their superiors or subordinates, and react in similar ways.

To get you thinking:

Motivation – subordinates

How do you motivate your subordinates? Arrange the following characteristics in rank order (1=high and 8-low) of priority.

Factor	Rank	Definition
High pay	_____	Paying them a salary which will enable them to improve their standard of living.
Advancement	_____	Giving them the opportunity to learn new skills or be promoted to more demanding jobs.
Pleasant companions	_____	Working with people who are friendly and approachable.
Autonomy	_____	Allowing them to set their own objectives (within your framework), to plan their day, and to have control over how they do their job.
Security	_____	Providing an assurance of continued employment and a comfortable retirement.
Responsibility	_____	Delegating decision-making and holding them accountable for results, including the control of resources.
Status	_____	Recognising the importance of their position in some non-monetary but tangible way.
Achievement	_____	Giving them the opportunity to solve problems and see the result of their efforts.

Motivation – subordinates: commentary

Most theories of motivation agree on a general order of importance for these motivation factors. Some of these factors are not controllable by the supervisor; for some the supervisor can have a significant input. This analysis and ranking (from High to Low) is based on Herzberg's Motivators and Hygiene Factors. This theory (it works!) is highly appropriate for use by supervisors.

- **Achievement (1)**

Supervisors can have a major input into this. They can create opportunities for people to actually achieve something important to themselves, to the team, to the job. The feeling of self-worth from this is enormous.

- **Advancement, Autonomy and Responsibility (=2)**

Again, the supervisor can have a major input into these factors. Certainly the supervisor can recommend promotion if the person has performed consistently well. Also the supervisor has control of working arrangements, which means that the levels of responsibility and autonomy can be arranged so as to give the individual the satisfaction of doing a job with little or no supervision, and producing a good result.

Although these are distinct characteristics, it is very difficult to disentangle them; they work together with each forming part of the other.

- **Pleasant companions (5)**

This is a low-level motivator and indeed is one of the factors that can cause a lot of dissatisfaction. It is one of the things that the supervisor can influence. If poor relationships are seen within the team, then the supervisor can step in and help sort things out.

- **High Pay (6)**

This is a low-level motivator and the supervisor has little or no influence on pay rates. Pay is never sufficient, and although raises are welcome, any incentive effect soon wears off.

Motivation and Expectations

- **Security and status (=7)**

Surprisingly, these two figure very little in the motivational scheme of things, and the supervisor has little influence. Security is mostly a contractual matter which we accept when entering the job. Status in a work situation rises with promotion; again we accept our position in the scheme of things. It is rare that status matters very much to people. However, respect and recognition do matter, but these should not be confused with a person's status or position, high or low, in the organisation.

If you are attempting to motivate your staff effectively, use the tools that you have some measure of control over. Organise tasks so that people get a sense of achievement from doing them; try to keep your supervision light and give plenty of sincere recognition.

16

Human Relations

'In war, three quarters turns on personal character and relationships; the balance of manpower and materials counts only for the remaining quarter.'
Napoleon I

Human relationships

Human relationships exist upwards, sideways and downwards, in business and in all walks of life. Knowing how to establish and maintain relationships is important to everybody; to a supervisor, it is absolutely vital.

The stages of a relationship

The first phase is **formation**; people meet for the first time and form an impression of one another.

Impressions tend to be formed quickly. They are sometimes based on very slight things. It is important during this phase (and every other one, come to that) to 'be yourself' in a natural, sincere and genuine way.

If everyone does this, then the next phase, **consolidation**, follows on steadily and naturally.

The speed of consolidation depends on the mix of personalities and the frequency and duration of contact. This phase is only difficult if, during the formation phase, the individuals concerned behaved in a non-natural way. It is impossible to disguise your real self for more than a very short time, so it is much better never to try.

The third phase is **preservation** (or its alternative, **deterioration**).

Well-consolidated relationships naturally preserve themselves. Others have to be preserved actively. It depends on the strengths of the bonds which hold the relationships together; these bonds, in turn, depend on how complementary the personalities of the individuals are.

Things which preserve relationships are loyalty, integrity, consistency, concern and communication. Things which destroy relationships are criticism, selfishness, insincerity, indifference, alterations in circumstances or interests and changes in personalities.

Action and reaction

People don't simply act according to their own intentions; they also react to the actions or words of others. It is hard to judge true reactions or feelings of other people; at times, we all think one thing and communicate another by words, expressions and body language.

To get on well with people, control your own reactions and predict how other people will respond to what you say and do. There are no reliable formulae for predicting how people will behave; all individuals are different.

The individual

No two people are alike. Any individual is a complex combination of many factors; in dealing with people, try to understand their make-up. Unexpected reactions may be caused by lack of understanding of an individual's make-up; if you understand the person, you have a much better chance of forecasting reaction and effect.

An individual is made up (amongst other things) of:

- personality, character, temperament
- financial and social position
- domestic situation, health, age
- employment, hobbies and interests, beliefs, academic abilities.

These factors do not remain static, therefore it is essential to be flexible when dealing with an individual.

Good human relationships are essential, for workplace success, and for personal happiness. A positive attitude towards life, concentrating more on the good things than on the bad things, and effective interpersonal communication will enhance human relationships.

'Good human relations' means:

- seeing things from the other person's point of view (empathy)
- remembering that all individuals are different
- thinking in terms of other people's needs and not just your own.

Do:

- communicate regularly, reliably and clearly with people
- give praise and appreciation where it's due (be careful of flattery!)
- behave naturally and genuinely
- say what you mean and mean what you say
- be loyal to your staff and your organisation
- be courteous to everyone
- admit when you're wrong
- show respect for everyone and express gratitude.

Don't:

- criticise harshly or destructively
- be tactless or hurt people's feelings
- lose your temper
- show impatience or intolerance
- be unpredictable
- short-circuit lines of communication.

Not surprisingly these 'Dos' and 'Don'ts' are very similar to the rules for good motivation practice, leadership and administration. Management must be treated holistically and although we have to study it one segment at a time, we have to try to encompass the whole in our everyday activity in getting the job done through people.

To get you thinking:

Human relations – How I rate myself

There isn't any real way that one can quantify human relationships, although relationships at work can be weighed up a bit more easily. Generally one has a feeling of being pleased or displeased, or feeling comfortable or uncomfortable, with ones' colleagues, either as individuals or as a group. This is obviously more or less intense, or you may be totally indifferent. Measuring this is problematical and subjective; but try.

Here is a list of characteristics of people or a group. Some are obvious and physical. Others are more emotional or behavioural. Now think about an individual, or some people with whom you work, and enter a one or two word comment, as you feel appropriate. To evaluate your feelings, use this list – write *yes, no, a little, a lot, never, always, sometimes*, or *usually* ...

- Do I like them?
- Am I influenced by what they look like?
- Do we communicate easily?
- Are there some things that they are not telling me?
- Are they supportive?
- Are they adaptable to my needs?
- Is it possible to negotiate with them easily?
- Do they load me with their own problems?
- Are their patterns of work (a.m. or p.m.) compatible?
- Are they compassionate?

Human Relations

- Do I feel comfortable with them? _____
- Do they make me feel uneasy? _____
- Are they flexible in their attitude? _____
- Do they have an awareness of the group's aims? _____
- Do they behave ethically? _____

Now put a tick (✓) as appropriate on the score card below. If you have 4 'Nos', your score is 4; if you have 3 'nevers', your score is 9 – and so on. Now read the commentary to see what you have told yourself.

	Value		Total
Yes	1	_____	
No	1	_____	
A little	2	_____	
A lot	2	_____	
Never	3	_____	
Always	3	_____	
Sometimes	4	_____	
Usually	4	_____	

Human relations: commentary

The list is an eclectic selection of characteristics; there are many more, but these concentrate on somewhat emotive elements, which tend to irritate!

If you have clocked up between 7 to 15 in the 'Yes' or 'No' lines you probably are not thinking too deeply around the ramifications of the statements.

A total of between 15 and 30 in the 'A little' and 'A lot' lines indicates that you are being somewhat tentative in your thinking about your relationships.

If you find that you have between 30 and 45 in the 'Never' and

'Always' lines, this will indicate that you have quite definite opinions about the people you work with; maybe not always complimentary ones either!

A score between 45 and 60 in the 'Sometimes' and 'Usually' lines are the realistic options. It is rare that we can make a definite hard cut statement about human relationships. People do behave like 'X' sometimes; they do behave like 'Y' usually. We cannot hope to systematise our human relationships, and the only thing that we can expect is the unexpected. Because people do not behave to rule, we need to be open on all sides and act and react in the most positive way possible.

17

Coaching

'Coaching is not a leaning post; coaching is for everybody, not just for the high flyer or problem cases.'

Peter Bolt

Coaching defined

Most people agree that coaching is a one-to-one process, involving direct, two-way communication and discussion:

Coaching is a process in which a supervisor, through direct discussion and guided activity, helps a colleague to learn to solve a problem, or to do a task better than would otherwise have been the case.

Coaching is concerned with improved task performance, and is central to improving the effectiveness of the organisation. Coaching helps to deliver the goods. Coaching is not a casual activity. It cannot be carried out without thought or attention. The effective coach needs a clear understanding of the process, together with a wide range of skills. Successful coaching requires a purposeful approach. Supervisors must know what they are trying to achieve, and why, and must be aware of what they are doing. The effective supervisor must take any opportunity to help colleagues to learn.

The coaching process

It is unrealistic to break down any process into separate stages. In practice, one bit of coaching merges into another, and into all the other things that go on between supervisors and their colleagues.

1. **Recognise the opportunity**
   Coaching opportunities arise from two different sorts of activity: the on-going work routine, and special assignments or job changes.

2. **Identify resources**
   Who can help? Maybe the supervisor has the time, skill and involvement to be the ideal person. But sometimes there is someone else in the organisation who could provide assistance more directly, with specific expertise.

3. **Set the climate**
   Some of the things that set a climate conducive to coaching are:

   - setting high performance standards
   - creating expectations for personal development
   - confirming that seeking help is OK
   - encouraging creative risk taking
   - encouraging learning from mistakes.

4. **Develop the helping relationship**
   Many actions can be built into the development of the learner. The diagram shows just some of the processes that surround the learner who is willing to accept coaching.

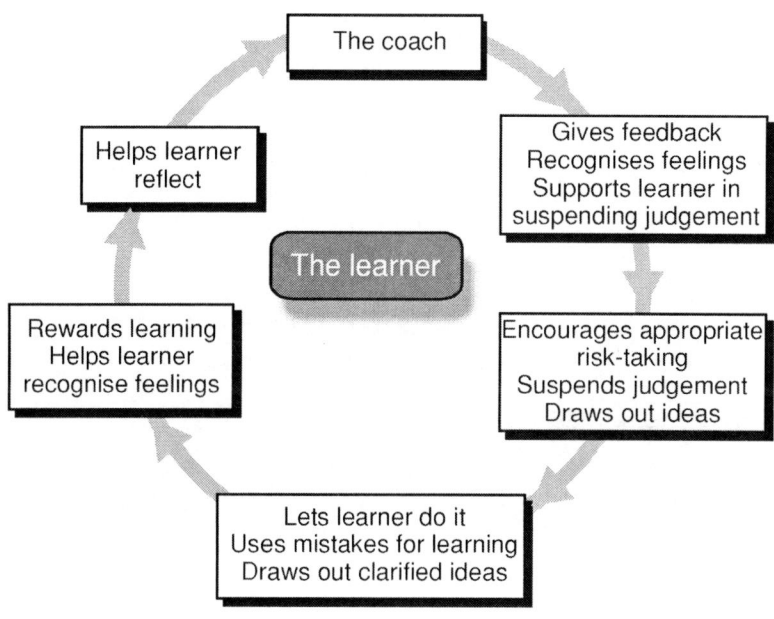

Figure 15 – The coaching process

5. Agree the plan

In a formal meeting, the coach and learner will need to establish a shared understanding of who will be responsible for what in the coaching process. This discussion also serves the purpose of clarifying expectations, as well as settling who does what.

6. Set goals and targets

There are two sorts of goals and targets to be considered:

- for the task to be performed
- for the learning to be achieved.

Who should be responsible for initiating and finalising goals and targets? This will vary from situation to situation. It may be that the balance of responsibility will be different with work goals than with learning goals.

7. Review work progress
It is important that the learner be as open as possible about the difficulties that they are encountering. The coach needs to use the skills of attending, suspending judgement, and giving feedback in helping the learner to be open about their difficulties. The goals and targets established provide a framework for this review. Other people involved in the work so far can be involved, if the learning climate is sufficiently positive for this to be practicable.

8. Provide help as necessary
The kind of help which is necessary depends very much on the nature of the task which is the focus of the coaching. The style, the timing and the way help is given will vary enormously.

Supervisors will be much concerned with providing supportive help early on, in the difficult stages of identifying the problem and generating solutions. At the later stage of presenting the findings, harder criticism may be appropriate. And at the implementation stage, often the most helpful thing a supervisor can do is to leave the learner to get on without help. The skills of not interfering and suspending judgement are highly important in many coaching situations.

Learners can get stuck with a problem and be reluctant to reveal this. The temptation for the coach is to come up with the solution to the learner's problem. This gives a feeling of competence and hopefully makes the learner grateful. Very often, however, such action does not solve the problem as the learner sees it, and can lead to resentment of the coach. Even if it does not cause resentment, help of this kind can generate dependency. In other words, next time the learner is stuck, rather than thinking things through for themselves, they will go straight to the coach for an instant solution.

The coach can ask a series of questions which give the learner a chance to solve most of the problem themselves. Such questions might be:

- What is the source of your problem?
- Can you identify blocks preventing you from solving the problem?
- Can you work on any of the blocks first?
- Do you need help with working on the blocks?
- How does the problem look now?
- What would things look like if the problem were solved?

By giving chances to review the problem, the coach may help the learners to come up with the solution themselves. If not, more direct suggestions from the coach may be appropriate.

9. Review learning

After the work goals have been attained, it is important that supervisor and colleague review the learning goals and targets. In working through them the supervisor should be sure that the colleague has not only thought through the implications of their learning for this occasion, but has also generalised to other situations which they may face in the future.

Bear in mind that no two people will perceive the same situation in the same way. So what a colleague learns will not be what the supervisor would have learned if they had been in the colleague's position. This fact emphasises the importance of asking what the colleague has learned, rather than telling them what they should have learned.

10. Confirm the new competence

If people acquire new competences, the most dispiriting thing that can happen to them is that they do not have a chance to practice it. So, make sure that the learners, who have learned how to do something new, continue to do it as often as is convenient. This confirms their skill, and fosters their own positive image of themselves, as learning, developing and growing people.

Coaching skills

There are skills which are especially important in coaching. None are particularly associated with any single stage in the coaching process, but are all part of the tool kit of a good coach, to be used as appropriate.

- **Attending**

Pay close attention to the learner. This shows respect, interest, care for both the learner and the problem. If the coach is clearly not paying attention, the learner will feel unimportant, and think that the coach would prefer to be doing something else, rather than wasting time.

Helpful attending behaviours:

- Sit facing the other person, without barriers in between.
- Maintain helpful eye contact; look directly at the other person, but without staring.
- Lean slightly forward towards the other person.
- Maintain a relaxed posture.
- Use encouraging responses: nodding, 'mming', saying 'Yes', 'I understand', 'I see what you mean' and so on.

This is all good 'Active Listening'.

- **Paraphrasing**

This is another form of attending behaviour. The listener repeats, in their own words, what they think the speaker has just been saying. Paraphrasing enables the listener to check that they are listening to the speaker; both hearing what is being said and being aware of the feelings. It also lets the speaker know that the listener is indeed listening.

Some guidelines for paraphrasing include:
- Listen carefully for the speaker's basic message; look out for non-verbal messages, the tone of voice, and sensing how they are feeling.
- Use your own words when paraphrasing what you think has

been said; do not act like a parrot and quote verbatim.
- If you lose the thread of what has been said, or do not understand, say so. If you do not follow the conversation do not pretend that you do.
- After paraphrasing, look for some sign from the speaker to tell you if your statement was accurate or inaccurate, or ask directly.

● Recognising and expressing feelings

Faced with a problem, an individual's feelings are involved. These may be about the problem itself; about some of the other people involved; about their own ability to solve it, and so on.

A skilful coach understands the importance of feelings, and how they may influence behaviour. It is important, therefore, to recognise how the other person is feeling, and be able to communicate. The first step to being truly comfortable with others' feelings is to be fully in touch with one's own. We express our feelings verbally, but more often communicate a great deal in this area non-verbally.

● Silence

Many of us are frightened by silence. We have the urge to say something, no matter what, in preference to silence. This need can be awkward in coaching situations; it can lead to over-hasty reaction and premature judgement. In order to maintain silence, it is useful to rerun the preceding exchanges over in your mind and keep an open, inviting expression on your face.

● Drawing out

It is useful to be able to 'draw out' the learner. This means getting him or her to talk about problems, feelings and ideas by using appropriate questions. Open questions are more effective at drawing out, than closed ones that may be answered by a 'yes' or 'no'.

Guidelines for asking drawing-out questions.
- Questions such as 'what?', 'why?' and 'how do you know?' tend to be open.
- If the learners talk only about facts, ask about their feelings.

- If they talk only about feelings, ask about the facts of the situation.
- If they talk in generalities, ask for examples.
- Questions that help to draw out *needs and objectives* include: 'What do you want to happen?', 'If everything went well, what would it be like?', 'Imagine the problem has been solved – what has happened?', 'What is the worst thing that could happen?', 'What is the best thing that could happen?', 'How would you feel then?', 'What would you do?'.
- Questions that help to draw out *ideas* include: 'What are all the relevant facts?', 'How do these facts relate to each other?', 'What alternative courses of action are open to us?', 'What will be the likely effect of each of these?'.
- Questions that help draw out *assumptions and thought processes* include: 'What makes you say that?', 'What happened to make you feel that way?'. 'What if ... (some other assumption)?', 'What other assumptions or conclusions would fit the facts better?'.

Drawing out is a very sensitive process. The coach must take care not to be too intrusive. At the same time, however, we really need to know what is going on, so a mild assertiveness is probably necessary.

● Giving and receiving feedback

One of the most difficult aspects of coaching is giving feedback – telling the other person your reactions to them and to their behaviour. Sometimes the coach wants to tell good things, at other times the feedback is negative. The problem in giving feedback is to do it in such a way that it is helpful. Often 'feedback' becomes 'slap-back', which usually has harmful effects to the relationship of both the parties involved.

Guidelines for giving feedback.
- Examine your motives for giving it.
- Feedback should be done at the time of the behaviour in question. It should not be postponed until it is too late.

- Feedback should be given when the learner is ready for it, and at an appropriate time.
- When giving feedback, describe the behaviour concerned, then give your reaction to it.
- Relate feedback to a specific piece of behaviour.
- Give feedback in terms of your reaction to behaviour.
- Ask for reactions to your feedback. Check that it has been understood. Make sure that you understand their feelings about it.
- Give feedback in small amounts. Do not overload.

The coach should also develop the skills of receiving feedback.

- Listen carefully to their description of your behaviour and their feelings about it.
- Give it careful consideration. Try to see the situation from the other person's viewpoint.
- Weigh up the pros and cons of changing or not changing your behaviour. Discuss these with the other person. Tell them your decision.
- You may need help to change your behaviour. Discuss this with them – particularly in so far as they can give you help (possibly by changing some of their own behaviour).

Coaching is, as you will have realised, a communication process that is focussed on learning needs. Any supervisor has as part of his or her (generally unwritten) job description a coaching role. This is inevitable; the supervisor knows the job, the subordinate may not. The supervisor needs good performance, so the subordinate has to find out how to do it well. Coaching is this process of finding out in a structured way and the supervisor has a major input into the learning process. Coaching is not teaching, it is learning; the difference in emphasis is important. Although the onus of imparting knowledge is on the supervisor, the responsibility for learning and performing is on the subordinate. The coach will have done a good job if the learner is able to carry out the tasks or functions acquired through coaching in an effective manner.

There is a good deal of satisfaction in successful coaching; it may be time consuming but supervisors should build coaching time into their time budget. Good results will lead to successful delegation, high motivation, improved productivity and thus profitability. All worth coaching for.

To get you thinking:

Your coaching style

Coaching successfully is not easy. It is challenging, may be uncomfortable, but gives powerful satisfaction when you see how people can enhance their behaviour and performance because of it.

As in everything in life (and management), there is no one way of doing coaching. What style you practice will be as a result of your own character and preferences. It is unlikely that you will adopt only one style; probably you will find that you combine several. Here we note some identifiable styles, with elements that combine to make up the overall style. See if you perceive your own style(s). Tick the boxes in this checklist that best describe you in the coaching role.

Teaching

The traditional role; active and directing and expecting compliance:

- ☐ Have expertise
- ☐ Good experience
- ☐ More talking than listening
- ☐ Collaborative
- ☐ Set patterns of imparting knowledge
- ☐ Patience
- ☐ Clarity of explanation
- ☐ Understanding of the learning process

Listening

Acting as a sounding board, and advisor, helping the learner to sort out their problems themselves:

- ☐ Providing a 'safe' place

- ☐ Empathy
- ☐ High level of concentration
- ☐ Active listening
- ☐ Keen questioning
- ☐ Commitment to the person

Supporter

Provides the enabling back up to help the learner implement ideas already thought out:

- ☐ Listening
- ☐ Empathy
- ☐ Analytical mind set
- ☐ Commitment
- ☐ Task focussed
- ☐ Emotional support
- ☐ Equal partnership

Parent

Something of an authority figure, directing the process rather more firmly than the Teacher. (It is not wise to use Parent mode too much; infrequent short bursts where needed to handle immature learners who may be reluctant to respond to other styles.)

- ☐ Show firmness
- ☐ Directing
- ☐ Telling what to do
- ☐ Not accepting giving up responsibility by the mentee
- ☐ Not granting permissions
- ☐ Not allowing dependency

Driver

Very firm, to deal with intractable problems. Shows concern, but straight-talking and focussed on what is going wrong and why:

- ☐ Negotiation
- ☐ Questioning directly
- ☐ Perseverance
- ☐ Clear sightedness
- ☐ Commitment to the individual

You will recognise parts of your own coaching style in all of these. Try to adopt the style(s) that are appropriate in the circumstances – the strategy that is most likely to work. But above all, be sincere and straightforward with your 'pupil'; there is no point in deceiving him, her or yourself, if you want positive results.

18

Conclusion

'Life is the art of drawing sufficient conclusions from insufficient premises.'
Samuel Butler

We have covered a lot of ground in this short book; all of the material is very relevant managerial knowledge for supervisors. Supervisors often get promoted into their new job, simply by knowing how, and doing, their own job very well. They are often unprepared and untrained for the managerial aspects of the work. This book has aimed to fill some of the knowledge needs. However, we cannot pretend that we have included every last item of management activity. There is much more, and the supervisor will discover by experience and by deliberately seeking out further information, how things work, and can be made to work – for themselves.

A brief review of what we have discussed

The concept of supervision, and the supervisor's job, were introduced and expounded. This led into an analysis of the idea of leadership and its relevance to the supervisor.

All management activity begins with planning – the process of deciding what has to be done and how to do it – result, a plan. For a plan to work, we need to ensure that what is supposed to happen happens – thus control. We also need to ensure that our resources – the team, are deployed to ensure that things do happen effectively.

Conclusion

The whole process is so intricately bound together that a failure in one area will inevitably affect the whole operation.

Problem solving is a major part of the supervisor's job. We offered a number of insights into problem solving, as well as several methods. However, it is not necessary to stick to any method slavishly. People should adjust their problem solving solutions to what works best for them. Pragmatic solutions are the key to successful problem solving.

We dealt with the main problem in business life (or in personal life for that matter!) how to use our time effectively. Good time usage is good management; having a plan and objectives is half the battle won. The other half is self-discipline and the knowledge of what is happening to our time, whether it is being used productively or is being wasted. Managing our time effectively is the key to success in the job; with good time management, all the other aspects of the supervisor's job slip into place.

Everyone feels uncomfortable with change; change to our working environment and practices most of all. It is the supervisor's responsibility to manage change, both the bosses and the staff expect this. We look at how this can be done. But once again one cannot manage change to a rigid formula. Each person will find that the theory is a framework on which to build his or her own pragmatic solutions.

Good delegation allows the supervisor to lighten burdens and enrich the job, as well as to develop subordinates. It is a difficult thing to manage to the satisfaction of all parties, but using the techniques described, the tasks can be done. The rewards of effective delegation are many, not least the motivational aspects which enhance the subordinate's job and enable the supervisor to deliver exceptional performance.

We all need to communicate and we do this in a wide variety of ways: speaking; writing; with body language; we talk at meetings, we make presentations, we talk on the phone; we record, the list is endless. We looked at some of the techniques we use and how we can make them more effective.

Motivation is the number one concern for the supervisor; well-motivated staff perform well. What turns people on – and off – is the subject of numerous theories and much writing. The ideas offered are straightforward and relevant for the supervisor. The supervisor's own motivation can be examined by exactly the same criteria, to see how well they themselves measure up in the basics of motivation. It is an essential topic, because supervisors who cannot motivate their staff are unlikely to do a good job.

The crucial subject is how we get on with people. Our relationships, particularly in the work situation, affect everything we do; we need to understand how they work and try to optimise them. Finally, the supervisor is the best placed to be a coach and is often called upon. How to do it well is part of tool kit of the effective supervisor.

In this book we have dealt with matters that are of direct relevance to any working manager/supervisor in the daily performance of his or her job. We have not included things which are outside of daily life, such as marketing, finance and so on, even though these are of course important. Our objective has been to concentrate on what matters the supervisor can influence. This has meant showing the importance of dealing with people properly, in order to manage any business effectively. We started out by stating that 'management is getting things done through people'. We close by hoping that this book has given the reader a little insight as to how that can be done effectively.

Further reading

Anyone wishing to further explore management theories and the ideas of management development will have a difficult time. The reason is that there is so much material, and more is being added daily (this book included). Many of the books and articles are dry as dust, academic treatises; other are crackpot expositions of arcane ideas which flourish and wither. Many are single ideas padded into an unreadable book; yet others are messianic texts proclaiming the one true way to solve all business problems.

Still there is a grain of truth in all of these and we have our own favourites which have influenced our thinking and development. I make no apology for the partiality of the following list. I have found most of them useful, idea rich, occasionally inspiring and above all (mostly) readable.

This is a personal list and there are few books originally published in the last couple of decades in it. That is not to say that there is nothing recent worth reading – of course there is. However, this list is dealing with fundamentals upon which later books on management theory tend to embroider. It is my belief that one needs to have a good foundation before going off on flights of fancy; this list will help build that foundation.

- John Adair – *The Effective Supervisor* – Industrial Society, 1988
- C. Argyris – *Understanding Organisation Behaviour* – Dorsey Press 1960
- Richard H. Axelrod – *Terms of Engagement* – Berret-Kohler 2000
- R. M. Belbin – *Management Teams* – Addison-Wesley 1981
- E. Berne - *Games People Play* - Deutch 1964
- S. Callis - *Good Writing for Business* – Chandos Publishing 2001

- John Casson – *Using Words* - John Casson 1977
- Edward de Bono – *Lateral Thinking for Management* – Penguin 1982
- Arle de Geus – *The Living Company* – Nicholas Brealey 1997
- Peter Drucker – *The Effective Executive* – Harper Row 1966
- F. E. Fiedler – *Leadership Effectiveness* – McGraw Hill 1967
- Saul Gellerman - *Motivation and Productivity* – A. M. A. 1963
- J. Gershuny – *Social Innovation* - O.U.P. 1984
- Charles Handy - *Understanding Organisations* - Penguin 1976
- J. Harvey-Jones – *Making it Happen* – Collins 1988
- Frederick Herzberg – *Work and the Nature of Man* – World Publishing 1966
- J. W. Humble – *Management by Objectives* – IER Foundation 1967
- J. Hurst – *Managing People at Work* – Pan 1981
- A. H. Maslow – *Motivation and Personality* – Harper Row 1954
- D. R. McGregor – *The Human Side of Enterprise* – McGraw Hill 1960
- Alec McKenzie – *The Time Trap* – McGraw Hill 1975
- H. Mintzberg – *Structuring Organisations* – Prentice Hall 1979
- Desmond Morris – *Manwatching* – Triad Panther 1978
- David O'Dell – Creative Problem Solving – Management Books 2000, 2001
- W. Ouchi - *Theory Z* – Addison-Wesley 1981
- C. N. Parkinson - *Parkinson's Law* – John Murray 1958
- Allan Pease – *Body Language* – Camel Publishing 1981
- Tom Peters & R. H. Waterman – *In Search of Excellence* - Harper Row 1982
- R. G. Revans – *Developing Effective Managers* – Longman 1971

Further Reading

- E. F. Schumacher – *Small is Beautiful* – Blond & Briggs 1973
- J. M. Thomas & W. G. Bennis – *Management of Change and Conflict* – Penguin 1972
- A. Toffler - *The Third Wave* – Pan 1981
- R. Townsend – *Up the Organisation* – Michael Joseph 1970
- W. F. Whyte – *Organisational Behaviour* – Irwin 1969
- W. H. Whyte – *The Organisation Man* – Doubleday 1957

Other books from Management Books 2000 Ltd

- Trish Nicholson – *52 Ways to Motivate Your Staff*
- Mike Pegg – *The Art of Mentoring*
- David McKeran – *Shaking the Tree* - New Thinking for Breakthrough Leadership
- John Chicken – *So You Want to Be a Manager?*

(See our website for the full list of 150 titles in our business and management range - www.mb2000.com)